A Kid's Kingdom

Growing Up in the City of Destiny

Also By Lance Lambert

Books

Gears, Grins & Gasoline: My Wheel Life Adventures
Fenders, Fins & Friends: Confessions of a Car Guy

On-Line & DVD

Custom Car Shows
Kings of Customizing
Classic Travel Trailers
Rat Rods & Traditionals
Dragsters to Duesenbergs
Odd Rods & Orphans
Motorhead Museums
Halls of Horsepower
Lowriders & Bombs
Drive-In Delights
Classic Dreams

DVD Boxed Sets

Classic Chrome
America's Classic Cars
America's Automotive Museums
Classic American Automotive Museums
American Classics Old School

Television & YouTube.com

"Vintage Vehicle Show" and VV Productions

A Kid's Kingdom

Growing Up in the City of Destiny

Lance Lambert

Wooded Isle Press

Requests for public readings by the author are encouraged.

A few of the stories in this book have previously appeared in various publications and on television & radio broadcasts. The author thanks *Garage Style Magazine, The Seattle Times, Nostalgia Magazine, Seattle Storytellers Guild, KBFG, The Moth Radio Hour* and additional publications, numerous on-line sites, and professional & trade publications for encouraging the inclusion of these stories in this book.

Photo & Graphic Credits: Tacoma Public Library, Richards Studio, Phyllis Lambert, Duane Vincent, MP-OTH Corp., Ed Roth Studios, Pro Films, NBC Television, Elizabeth Kiteley, Rex. F. Adams Co., Dave Daily, Etiquette Records, Buck Ormsby, Toppers Car Club, Dick Page, Chuck Naubert, Sue Elrod, Rosewood Photography, Jini Dellaccio, Dick Clark Productions, Erik Timothy, Joe Sexton, Continental Baking Company, Lance Lambert and a few people that posted photos on the internet without credit or contact information.

Published and printed in the United States of America

Cover Design: Tomo Kuman-Lesher, Visual Solution + Organization

ISBN-13: 978-0-692-88345-7

Wooded Isle Press, 2400 NW 80th St., #272, Seattle, WA 98117

To my grandson Cale

Don't try to do everything that Bapa did, but be sure to do some of it.

Foreword

When you look up "nostalgia" in the dictionary, I'm pretty sure you'll find a photo of Lance Lambert. People in the classic car community know Lance from his 24 years of hosting television's *Vintage Vehicle Show* and from his two books of short car stories that are delightful drives down Memory Lane. With this collection of stories, Lance turns his dual powers of keen observation and off-kilter insight onto his childhood in America's greatest small city – T-Town – Tacoma, Washington, *The City of Destiny*.

I met Lance in an improv class in the early 1990s and was astounded by his quick wit and sense of the absurd that had me wiping away tears of laughter. Lance was never one of those funny people who uses put-down humor, shaming, name-calling or any other kind of cruelty to get a laugh. Lance simply perceives with clarity, and reminds us of the details of life, the small moments we've all experienced and pretty much forgotten – and he brings these universal recollections into the light of warm affection so we can take part in a shared appreciation for the ridiculousness and precariousness of life.

That's not to say that Lance's life was a charmed one with abundant blessings. He shares stories of childhood sleep disorders, coming from a "broken home" (his parents divorced), and scrambling to earn money through odd jobs and collecting glass bottles because, as his mother told him, "I have no money for clothes for you, so you'll have to find the money to buy anything you need." For Lance, this wasn't a source of shame or despair – just a statement of fact, and he set off to find the money to buy a pair of shoes.

Lance reveals the preferred method of eating Hostess SnoBalls (purchased for almost free at the Wonder Bread Bakery Thrift Store), exposes the yearning for popularity in high school that resulted in joining in a dubious social club, and divulges the privilege of staying up late to watch Jack Paar on *The Tonight Show* with his "worldly and sophisticated" older sister who made Saltines and Velveeta Cheese seem like a gourmet delight. And, of course, there is his love affair with cars. Anything with wheels. Also, a developing interest in "humans of the opposite gender."

Lance's stories are achingly truthful, often laugh-out-loud funny, and generous in spirit. I think Lance best describes his unique take on the world in the story titled *Tears in the Tunnel* when he says, "For most of my life, friends and relatives have accused (complimented) me of being 'sensitive.' Not the 'You hurt my feelings' kind of sensitivity. It is more the type of sensitivity that is struck by the beauty of something, be it nature, art or just an act of kindness."

A Kid's Kingdom: Growing Up in the City of Destiny is an act of kindness to us, the lucky readers of Lance's tales of growing up in Tacoma in the soft black-and-white shades of the 1950s and 1960s. The *Happy Days* of the Fonz and *American Graffiti*. But also with some not-so-happy events endured by a sensitive boy with a gift for tender storytelling and a well-oiled funny bone. Tacoma is truly, for him, *The City of Destiny*. And his destiny was to write lovingly about his childhood and teenage years in T-Town.

M.J. McDermott
Meteorologist, KCPQ, Q13 News, Seattle
Author of *The Improv* and *Frankenstein Meets Santa*

Contents

Author's Note

"The past beats inside me like a second heart." John Banville

The incidents and activities described in this book cover a time period (circa 1950-1965) from my preschool years to the humiliating party after my high school graduation ceremony. A few of the stories have been published in two previous books: *Fenders, Fins & Friends: Confessions of a Car Guy,* and *Gears, Grins & Gasoline: My Wheel Life Adventures.* Some of the stories have also been published in various magazines, newspapers and on-line publications. To these outlets I extend my gratitude for their support and encouragement in the writing of this and previous books.

In the other books I referred to my brother—a recurring character in my life's story—as Jay. His full name is Lynn Jay Lambert, and he was called Lynn by everyone well into his adult years, when he decided to take on his middle name as his preferred moniker. I have chosen to use his first name of Lynn throughout this book because that is what he was called at the time that the activities shared here took place.

The names in the stories are the actual names of the people described. I contacted several of them to verify various facts and they gave me permission to use their names. I was able to contact most of the people involved, but a few didn't respond to my inquiries. However, all of the people in the book are described favorably and will, I hope, be flattered by my observations, descriptions and comments. All embarrassing revelations pertain to my own actions, so I should be the plaintiff in any resulting litigation.

Readers, including both friends and strangers, frequently ask the question, "How do you remember so much from your past?" The simple answer is that I just do; however, I've had some assistance.

My mother was an amateur photographer and took many of the photographs seen in my books. Every glance at a photo refreshes my memories of family, friends and activities that are now preserved in grainy black & white or faded color. From Mom I picked up the habit of frequently taking a camera with me to record various daily activities with my teammates-in-life.

I'm also a personal history hoarder. Displayed in my garage is a brick from Franklin Elementary School, the location of a few stories in this book. From Stadium High School I still have the mug I made in Mr. Westlin's art class. In one of my many scrapbooks are the Stadium High School "activity cards" used to get into dances and sports events, and the ticket from the Class of 1965 graduation ceremony. A cherished item is the piece of paper upon which my wife, when I met her over forty years ago, wrote her phone number.

How far back and how accurately do I recall the activities in my life?

From my birth until I was two, my family lived in a small home located in the Salishan neighborhood of Tacoma, WA. This area consisted of modest homes built during WWII to house military families. I still remember the home like I was there yesterday. Many decades ago my mother questioned my memory and doubted, since I was only two years old when we moved, that I could remember anything about the house. I surprised her by drawing an accurate floor plan of the structure.

The mist of time may have added a rose-colored tint to some memories, but to the best of my knowledge the ones I've shared in this book are accurate and truthful. Sharing them puts a smile on my face and, occasionally, brings a tear to my eyes. It is my hope that you share the smiles and understand the tears.

Lance Lambert

The Lamberts 1957 – Judy, Lynn, Rex, Lance, Phyllis

Tacoma, Washington

Tacoma adopted its name after the nearby Mount Rainier, originally called Takhoma and Tahoma. Tacoma was chosen to be the western terminus of the Northern Pacific Railroad in 1873 and, as a result, the local citizens proudly proclaimed Tacoma to be *The City of Destiny.*

Morning Bugs

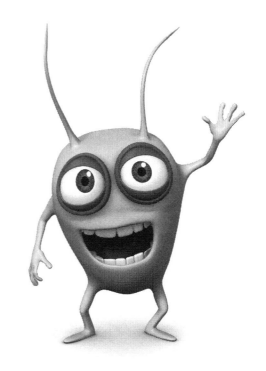

Some children have an invisible friend. The friend may be an understanding child, a supportive adult or a loving animal. My invisible friend was a bug; a very tiny bug almost too small to see. Actually, it was millions of tiny bugs almost too small to see.

Waking up early has been a pattern my entire life. Even during my childhood and young-adult years I frequently woke up earlier than my siblings and parents. Friends would talk of "sleeping-in" until mid morning and I'd respond that often it was still dark outside when my peepers popped open and my feet sought out my slippers.

Frequently at bedtime or upon wakening I would rock back-and-forth while sitting up in bed. These days a child displaying this action is referred to as having *Rhythmic Moving Disorder*. Back then it was just a kid sitting up and rocking in bed. I found it soothing and it seemed to lull me to sleep at night and gently wake me in the morning. An unintended by-product is that it also caused my bed to move an impressive distance across the bedroom floor. I don't recall my parents being concerned about that and, here's the best part: this "disorder" brought me physically closer to my invisible friends. Let me explain.

When I ask other people what they see upon waking in the morning, what they describe is identical, or at least very similar, to what I see. As day breaks and darkness is slowly replaced by light, the world around me looks physically "grainy." By that I mean that everything seems to be made up of nearly imperceptible "specks" that range from light gray to black. A good illustration is the graininess seen in black and white photographs utilizing film, especially, for photography geeks, Kodak Tri-X 400 film. I was very aware of these grains as daylight slowly arrived each morning.

Often, at the time I was awakening, it was still dark or the sun was just barely coming up over the horizon. The location of my bed, by now, due to the rocking, was about 3 to 5 feet closer to the bedroom window than where it sat the night before. This provided me a front row seat to the arrival of my favorite friends--the bugs.

To my child's eyes, the "graininess" I mentioned above appeared to be tiny bugs that filled the air everywhere I looked. Perhaps some children might be frightened by this vision, but I was not because these bugs were there to do something good for me. They had arrived to eat the darkness.

I thought these bugs came every morning to gobble up the darkness so the people could begin their days and be able to see the world around them. Each minuscule bug would eat a minuscule amount of darkness and, being so hungry and so plentiful, before long all of the darkness was eaten and the sun was either lighting up the sky or sending sunlight through the clouds.

I would speak to the bugs, expressing my appreciation to them for performing this daily duty.

The bedroom window was draped with curtains that had a cowboy and Indian motif. Printed on the fabric were stagecoaches, horses, covered wagons, bare-chested warriors with bows & arrows, rifle toting cowpokes in big hats, and lots of cactus and sagebrush. All of these dusty and leather adorned characters and horse drawn transportation modes seemed to be moving in my mind's eye as I stared at the material. The woven wild-west show became clearer and brighter as the friendly bugs progressed in their daily job. In no time the dark was completely consumed and the bugs moved on to the next town that needed its darkness devoured.

As the years passed I took the bugs for granted and the bed (nocturnal stagecoach?) stopped transporting me into the sunrise. Eventually, of course, I realized that there were no bugs eating the darkness. But even now, the imaginative child in me thanks these tiny friends.

Tears in the Tunnel

Like most little boys, I loved both trains and Santa Claus. So I was lucky that in my town there was a "real" train just the right size waiting to take little boys and girls on a journey to the North Pole to meet Santa.

Rhodes Department Store was Tacoma's answer to Macy's Department Store. It was my family's opinion that this was the classy place to shop for the city's well-to-do. We were only well off enough to perhaps buy socks and underwear there, but the big draw for us was "window shopping" throughout the store. A few times a year I'd accompany my mother as she strolled the aisles taking in all the latest styles that were the current rage in New York, Los Angeles and even nearby Seattle.

Rhodes Department Store

One of the exciting things offered at Rhodes was a train that was set up every Christmas season. This was a small functioning train that was large enough to carry four children in each of the four passenger cars that were pulled behind the engine. The train, though a miniature, was a very realistic replica of the Milwaukee Railroad's Hiawatha that, according to the information given by the store, traveled between Spokane, Washington and Great Falls, Montana. An added stop, at least for this miniature train, was the North Pole, where the passengers could visit Santa. The sign above the loading platform said the passengers were leaving from the town of "Hiawatha Ville" and another sign stated that the elevation was 63 feet and the population was 18.

Children would line up and then, with the aid of a uniformed conductor and an engineer, climb aboard the train and travel to Santa's workshop. As the train left the station it entered a long curved tunnel with Saint Nick waiting at the other end with a warm knee to sit on and a candy cane to take home.

My mother, during this particular holiday season in the early 1950s, decided that I would like to take a ride on this train to visit Santa. I was four or five years old at the time, and riding a train to the North Pole, sitting on Santa's knee, making a few gift requests and then riding the Hiawatha back into my mother's arms seemed like a great way to spend some time. The likelihood of getting derailed in a snowstorm or avalanche in Rhodes Department Store was remote, and the likelihood of getting a candy cane from Santa was excellent. This all seemed like a good thing to both Mom and me. Things didn't turn out quite as well as we'd planned.

For most of my life friends and relatives have accused (complimented) me for being "sensitive." Not the "You hurt my feelings" kind of sensitivity, but more of the type that finds me struck by the beauty of something, be it nature, art or just an act of kindness. Sometimes this sensitivity manifests itself inappropriately or at a time when it should be repressed, and sometimes, as it was on this day, it is completely misunderstood by others.

There my mother and I stood waiting for the train to return and the young passengers to disembark and make room for me and my fellow riders to head for the North Pole. I let go of her hand, walked to a waiting car and made myself comfortable. Soon the train left Hiawatha Ville and we entered the tunnel on our way to Santa Town. This was my first (and last) ride on the Hiawatha.

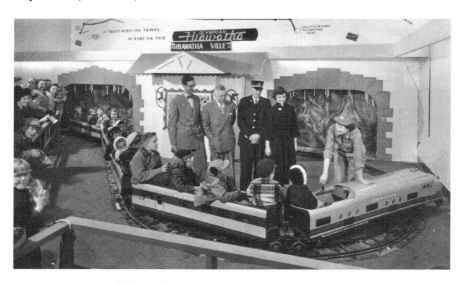

The Hiawatha leaving the station

The interior of the tunnel was covered with crumpled tinfoil and sparkled with various colors from the spinning multicolored lights along the track. It was absolutely beautiful. This experience took place 65 years ago but my mind's eye still sees it as if the train ride was taken last week. The tunnel's interior may have been the most beautiful thing that I had ever seen at that point in my young life.

Here's where the sensitive part comes into play. I was so overwhelmed by the beauty that, even at four or five years of age, tears began forming and rolling down my cheeks. Soon a river of tears were flowing and I began crying like...like an overwhelmed four- or five-year-old kid.

It appeared that I was the only slobbering kid onboard. The tears caused by beauty were interpreted as tears caused by fear, so the engineer decided to stop the train mid-tunnel. The conductor plucked me from the passenger car, walked me out of the tunnel and requested that the appropriate mother claim her little crybaby. She was probably very sympathetic and a little embarrassed. I was humiliated, embarrassed and frustrated that my tears were not understood. I was not mature enough, articulate enough or confident enough to explain why I was crying.

I was not afraid! It was the crumply tinfoil and cheap colored lights that got to me. They were magnificent!

I do not recall if we left the Rhodes Department Store while avoiding eye contact from strangers, or if we continued strolling through the various departments. I'm sure my mother comforted me and told me everything was fine. She didn't, however, take me back to the Hiawatha train station the following Christmas season.

Catastrophe in the Closet

I had a pretty good older sister. She was very supportive, always upbeat and included me in some of her more grown-up activities. Judy was seven years older and sometimes took on the role of a parent rather than a sibling. I didn't mind, and occasionally was grateful. She was even forgiving when I did something that most siblings would not quickly forgive.

Big sister Judy

As a child I had a few sleep disorders. I rocked back-and-forth in bed so vigorously that my bed would move across the floor a few feet. I was a bed wetter several years past what is considered acceptable. And on at least one occasion I lost my sense of direction, resulting in a hygiene mishap that became a legend in our family. I'll tell that story in a moment, but first I have to explain about the closets.

Our home, though moderate in size, had large closets. Each bedroom had a walk-in closet that could actually be walked into, and the closet in my bedroom was the largest of them all. It was so large that it could be used as a small room, and I often pretended that it was an office. I setup my little table and chair, along with a bookcase, and imagined that I was an important businessman sitting in his private office. The closet was large enough to accommodate the furniture, my clothes, and still have space to lie down and hide between the hanging clothes and an outside window. That closet provided me with the feeling of either being very important, or of being hidden from my family. It was a great closet.

Mom and Dad's closet was stuffed with clothes, boxes, shoes and hanging belts and ties. But it was the most appealing closet in the house for one reason: Marilyn Monroe was in that closet.

Marilyn, pretty much at the top of her game when I was a kid, was too busy to actually spend time in my parent's closet. She was there, however, in all of her splendor. Yes, *all* of her splendor!

One of Marilyn Monroe's most famous publicity photographs consists of a very revealing image of her stretched out across a large piece of red satin. The majority of her best attributes were available for viewing in this famous photo. A calendar was hanging in Mom and Dad's closet that displayed this photograph. During my pre-teen years there were many times when I entered that closet with the goal of increasing my knowledge of the female anatomy.

My brother's closet was a bit smaller and smelled like a brothel, or at least a testing room for the Old Spice Company. Lynn always liked to dress nicely and that included wearing ironed shirts. He would carefully iron a shirt and then wear it to school or a special event. What he didn't like to do was repeat the ironing after the shirts were washed, so he came up with a solution: just keep wearing them. He would be careful not to soil them and then, upon returning home, take off the shirt, spray deodorant in the armpit area and hang it up. The result was that his closet emitted a strong odor similar to that of a sailor at the end of a weekend pass. To his credit he always looked well-dressed and smelled better than most of the other teenage boys in the neighborhood.

My sister Judy's closet was the smallest in the house, but it still was a walk-in that featured hanging storage on either side of the door. Apparently I thought it was very similar to the family's bathroom. Thus, the family legend I mentioned earlier.

Lynn's, Judy's and my bedrooms were on the second floor and the home's only bathroom was on the first floor. The staircase from our bedrooms down to the first floor was skinny and a bit steep. No matter, if I had to go to the bathroom I would stumble down the stairs, take care of business and climb sleepily back up the stairs. It was a simple procedure that the three of us had done hundreds of times. But on one occasion, apparently, I forgot the procedure.

That night I woke up and needed to go to the bathroom, so I commenced the steps necessary to relieve the need, technically known in the medical community as "having to go number one." The usual path was to exit my bedroom door, proceed straight ahead, walk down the stairs, take a quick left and a quick right, complete number one and then return to my bedroom by reversing the previous steps. However, on this particular night my toilet radar (toildar?) was not functioning properly.

I climbed out of bed, walked out the bedroom door, took a hard left, walked a short distance, took a hard right and entered my sister's closet. Totally left out was the going down the stairs part of the usual procedure. I then pulled down my pajama bottoms, took out my number one apparatus and created a small lake on my sister's closet floor.

The temporary shine on her shoes reflected the 40 watt bulb above beautifully.

As I mentioned earlier in this story, Judy was a good sister. On this night during this mishap she once again showed how understanding and supportive she could be.

As her sleepy baby brother stood there peeing freely on her shoe rack she asked the reasonable question, "What are you doing?"

To me it seemed a silly question and, even sillier, why was she standing in the bathroom asking me what I was doing. It's the bathroom. I'm going to the bathroom. Isn't that obvious?

Two things happened at this moment. I began to realize that there were a bunch of clothes hanging up in the bathroom that had not been there a few hours earlier. Also there was no toilet where very recently there had been a toilet.

I was not the smartest of the Lambert siblings, so what had just happened slowly started to become clear to me. It appeared that I was actually peeing in my sister's upstairs closet instead of the downstairs bathroom.

I was confused, but my sister, thankfully, was very understanding about something that not many people would likely understand. She let me finish my business and then gently walked me back to my bedroom.

The following day there was no anger, teasing or request to help clean up the mess from the previous night. The incident was not discussed again for a long time. After a decade or two, however, we began sharing the catastrophe in the closet story when we got together. We laughed about it, but when I visit her, I always make sure that my toildar is functioning properly and, when nature calls, that I arrive at the correct destination.

Kissing Mary Kay

Mary Kay was blond, pretty, and recently she and I had exchanged many smiles. Perhaps we were two 7-year-olds made for each other.

Franklin Elementary School was a typical middle America grade school. Built in the 1920s, the brick structure consisted of classrooms, halls lined with lockers, a basement expansive enough for typical indoor sports, with four-square and dodge ball being our most popular games. At the rear of the school was a covered play area, a playfield large enough for two baseball fields, and a separate playground area on either side of the school, one side for the girls and the other side for the boys. Each side had its own swing set. I'm not sure why we couldn't share the same swing sets, but no doubt it had something to do with dresses rustling in the breeze and boys being quick to giggle. Whatever the reason, this division was not going to stop my pursuit of the lovely Miss Mary Kay O'Reilly.

Mary Kay was the daughter of the butcher at Heckel's Thriftway store. I met her when we were both in kindergarten and, at that time, I was under the impression that her family was very wealthy. This was based on knowing that all doctors were wealthy and therefore butchers, also working with body parts, must have the same knowledge and expertise as any doctor and, again therefore, must be wealthy. This meant that Mary Kay was both pretty and had lots of money. Wealth meant to me that she lived in a mansion and had an abundance of good food, and probably was able to eat hamburgers every day, or at least for breakfast and dinner. The sack lunch she carried to school likely contained cold hot dogs, or boloney with pimento olives, a true delicacy only enjoyed by rich people.

So what I'm looking at is a pretty girl, unlimited beef and chicken byproducts delights, and a school with a strict rule that boys and girls do not to set foot in each other's play area. There was an area between the two playgrounds that was heavily supervised by teachers with the sole purpose of making sure the miniature members of the opposite sex did not have any physical contact other than throwing rubber balls at each other.

Mary Kay and I were both in the first grade and, although we were quite young to have any romantic interest, we had taken a liking to other when we first met as kindergarteners. Little did we know then that our mutual interest would result in the first experience of a real kiss, not a sending-you-off-to-school kiss from a loving mother or a holiday smooch from an odd-smelling and overly expressive aunt.

Communication between the opposite sexes was hampered by the playfield design and rules. If a boy walked up the short incline to the girls' play area he would immediately be scolded by a teacher and told to return to the real estate meant to be occupied by boys. Upon returning to the designated boys' area the youngster who had ventured onto the wrong end of the playground would likely be subject to ridicule.

"Where's your dress? Shouldn't you be wearing a dress if you want to play with the girls?" Other taunts would be tossed and the trespasser would not likely err again.

It was different for the girls. None of them seemed to want to be anywhere near the boys' area, with the exception of Mary Kay O'Reilly. She was a brave little girl.

It was during a visit by her onto the boys' turf when I spotted the blond hair shining in the sunlight. I was vigorously swinging back and forth on the swing set when she approached the boys' area.

There was a small basketball court in front of the swings that she was crossing. The benefit of this court was that, if you swung hard enough and jumped far enough, you could eject from the swing and land on the asphalt court rather than on the dirt and sawdust mixture that was under the swings. The successful departure from the swing seat, followed by landing on the asphalt court without breaking any bones, assured the admiration of all those who observed the successful flight. The experience of my first kiss was preceded by such a flight and a landing worthy of any Ringling Brothers Circus act.

I was swinging as hard and high as physics would allow, sure that with just a little more effort I'd be able to swing so hard that a 360-degree circle would be the result. It was so high that the tallest chapels in Mexico City were nearly in view. OK, I'm exaggerating a bit, but I was swinging hard and riding high. It was then that the top of Mary Kay's head came into view.

What was she doing on our side of the playground? Didn't she know the rules? Wait, is she looking up at me and smiling? She was, and she continued displaying her Irish smile in my direction. I'd seen this kind of communication between grownups on television, but not in real life.

It was then that I made the decision to make a lasting impression on the rich butcher's beef-fed daughter. I decreased my swinging arc just a little, scooted forward a few inches on the canvas seat and prepared to eject. This would, no doubt, impress Mary Kay O'Reilly and be a great conversation starter.

It was time to take flight and prepare for the happy

landing. If all went well I'd land on the asphalt court as impressively as any return to terra firma by every child's hero, Superman. Mary Kay would be my Lois Lane and she'd swoon with admiration as my muscular first grader's body came to an abrupt stop next to her. If my landing failed I'd either be standing in a cloud of dirt and wood dust like a mere kindergartener, or I'd be picking out asphalt bits from my fresh wounds.

The angels hovering over the playground protected me that day. I landed next to Mary Kay as solidly and dramatically as any superhero. Yes, she seemed to be very impressed.

My athletic prowess provided the opportunity for the beginning of a conversation that probably was quite sophisticated for two first graders.

"Um, hi." I said, nearly breathless from my death-defying leap up into and down from the sky.

"Um, hi." She replied, brushing back a blond bang, just like the ladies did in the movies.

"Um, you wanna, um sit over there?" I said, pointing to a nearby window ledge.

"Um, OK." She replied as we began walking side-by-side.

The conversation then likely included discussions of various meat product surgeries performed by her father, and if my leaping ability might result someday in me being either a professional skydiver or famous circus performer. The conversation continued and, unknown to either of us, the moment of our first kiss drew near.

I do not remember the exact moment, but do remember the exact place and posture. We stood up next to the window closest to the swings, leaned forward and kissed. It may have just been a quick and innocent kiss, but it was intentional by both of us and was a genuine lips to lips kiss. I probably closed my eyes like the people did in the movies, and perhaps even made a loud smacking sound with my lips. Whatever our lips did, I knew that I liked it!

The exchange was not followed by an engagement or any wedding plans. There was not even a second kiss. The passionate part of our relationship lasted just the one- or two-second duration that our lips touched. We didn't become "a couple" at this point either. I don't think it is possible to do that until you are at least in junior or senior high school. There may have been a time or two of walking home together, and maybe even a complimentary slice or two of pimento baloney from her father when I was inspecting the latest candy shipment to Heckel's Thriftway.

Mary Kay and I are still friends, and we laughed about that first kiss experience recently when we both attended our 50th high school reunion. As we shared the story I could not help but notice that she is still blond and still pretty. I didn't have the courage to ask her if she became wealthy after inheriting all of her father's millions from his butcher practice.

The butcher's daughter and author in 2015

Eisenhower and Lincoln

It was a cold October morning in 1956 when the President of the United States drove by my grade school.

Dwight D. Eisenhower was near the end of his first term as President and was touring the country attempting to gather votes enabling him to remain in office for another term. I was 9 years old at the time and just another kid attending Franklin Elementary School. The usual daily routine at school was going to be changed significantly on that day because the President of the United States was scheduled to drive by. *THE PRESIDENT OF THE UNITED STATES*! My school! This was a big deal for me and all of the other residents of Tacoma.

The school's students were asked to dress nicely for the event. My usual clothing routine was to put on a clean outfit on Monday and wear the same clothes to school all week. Looking back that seems like a bad plan, but at the time it was normal in the Lambert home, at least for me. The day of the President's visit was a Thursday (thank you internet) but I decided that wearing a clean outfit and breaking the Lambert dress code would be OK since, after all, the guy was the President.

The big day arrived and our teachers marched us out of the school and down the street to Franklin Park that adjoined the school. There we stood on the sidewalk, along with hundreds of older citizens, waiting for the official motorcade to pass by.

After a short time I glanced down the street and saw a few important looking cars coming toward me and my classmates. The second or third car back was a very unusual looking vehicle. The year, as I said, was 1956, but some of the official presidential vehicles in use at the time were manufactured a few years earlier. Coming down the street was a huge 1950 Lincoln convertible with *THE PRESIDENT OF THE UNITED STATES* waving at the people lined up on the sidewalk! Right there in front of me was *THE PRESIDENT*, in my neighborhood, driving by my school! This was back when citizens had respect for the office of President, even if they didn't agree with the office holder's politics.

The impact of seeing such a massive and beautiful car was enough to bring tears to my eyes, and seeing the President waving from the car assured that the tears would flow. Then it happened: *THE PRESIDENT OF THE UNITED STATES OF AMERICA WAVED AT ME!* There I stood, no doubt looking splendid in my clean first-day-of-the-week school clothes, and passing by me in the beautiful 1950 Lincoln was *THE PRESIDENT OF THE UNITED STATES* looking right at me and waving! There was only one thing that I could do: Yes, I waved back and then began bawling like a little kid. I guess that was OK since I was 9 years old and still a little kid.

I have no memory of being embarrassed or creating any kind of a scene that was noticed by anyone. Everyone was probably feeling a bit emotional too, so some tearful kid at the side of the road likely did not draw any attention.

The anticipation was long but the arrival and departure of the motorcade was brief. Our teachers then hurried us back into the school and we returned to our classrooms to resume, as best we could, a normal day.

President Dwight D. Eisenhower in a 1950 Lincoln

The impact of seeing the President was great, and the impression made by the 1950 Lincoln was nearly as great. The car was a huge luxury convertible fitted with everything needed to make the President comfortable. The President, in turn, made most of the citizens in the country feel comfortable. No wonder he was successful in his reelection campaign. Looking back, I still think Eisenhower was one of our better commander-in-chiefs.

It was a great day when I got to see the President up close and personal. How could it be anything other than great when a very good President rides by in a car named after another very good President?

Kids and Cash

In the 1950s and 1960s the kids in my neighborhood all shared approximately the same lifestyle and standard of living. Our dads left for work five days a week, most of our moms worked seven days a week at home and we all lived in what was considered a middle to lower middle class neighborhood. It seemed normal to all of us kids, including the fact that we never had much money to spend. I was not aware of any friends ever going hungry or not having decent clothes to wear, but nobody had much more than the basics. I didn't receive an allowance, so I needed to find a way to acquire some spending money. Fortunately, a few opportunities were made available for the neighborhood's children to make a few cents and perhaps even a few dollars.

Most of my friends growing up were active at the local YMCA, officially known as the Young Men's Christian Association. I learned to swim in the local "Y" pool and learned the game of pool on one of the YMCA's pool tables. The organization also provided another activity that appealed to me: going to Camp Seymour. This was a summer camp where young boys could spend a week doing everything expected at an outdoor camp: going boating and swimming, shooting with bows and arrows, throwing horseshoes, and sitting around the campfire while singing, "Seymour will shine tonight, Seymour will shine. When the sun goes down and the moon comes up, Seymour will shine...."

Spending a week at the camp was not free and my

parents let me know that there was no extra money in the family budget to pay for their youngest child to shoot arrows into trees and toss rocks at other kids passing by in rowboats. Fortunately, the YMCA provided a way to make the necessary money: selling bars of soap door-to-door.

I was 8 years old and had never done anything door-to-door other than knocking on one and asking if Dale, Jimmy, Frankie or Johnny could come out and play. Knocking on a door with the intent of exchanging a product for cash was a new experience for me, although it didn't sound too difficult.

After a trip to the YMCA and back home, my bed was covered with large boxes filled with a lot of small packages, each containing a bar of soap. I was struck with how similar they looked to neatly lined up packs of cigarettes. I had the soap; now it was time to learn to be a salesman (salesboy?).

Saturday morning arrived and out the door I went carrying a large box filled with small bars of soap. First stop was the home of Mrs. Dahl's, the "sweet little old lady" living next door, to ask if she wanted to buy some soap. My mother had helped me practice a short sales pitch so I was prepared to make my first sale. Mrs. Dahl loved me and my siblings and she would have happily bought dead rodents if that was what I was selling. If memory serves me correctly, the bars of soap were 25 cents each, which looking back might have been a little expensive. The sales pitch let potential customers know their purchase would make it possible for the little guy on the porch to go to camp, and no decent person would want to deprive anyone of this important part of growing up in America.

In a couple of Saturday afternoons I sold all of the soap necessary for me to see Camp Seymour shine for five nights.

The following summer provided a different opportunity to see more of Camp Seymour. This time the source of income was not provided by the YMCA. Instead of selling soap for the outside of the body I sold something for the inside of the body: donuts. More specifically, I became a door-to-door "Spudnut" salesman. This was a donut made with potato flour, thus the name Spudnut. Who knew flour could be made from a potato and then used to create a donut?

MORE AND MORE PEOPLE ACROSS THE NATION ARE ACCEPTING THE CORDIAL INVITATION TO

Meet Mr. Spudnut

COAST TO COAST ..
ALASKA TO MEXICO

SPUDNUTS*

America's Finest Food Confection

Spudnuts were available across the country from various bakeries that had a franchise to sell it. All I remember about them is that they were big, glazed and easy to sell. At 9 years old I still had the cute little boy look, so no mom could resist buying a donut or two from the cherry-cheeked kid standing on her front porch.

"Do you want to buy a Spudnut? If you do then I will be able to go to summer camp."

With that sales pitch and my freckles, the chance of any resistance to handing me a dollar or two melted. Selling donuts was easier than selling soap, and the leftover crumbs in the bottom of the box tasted much better than the ones the soap left.

Another method of making some spending money was to pick up the hard, cold cash that was lying all around. It was hard and, much of the time, it was also cold because the "cash" was made of glass.

Beer bottles and soda bottles were worth money. Recycling back in the 1950s meant that the beverage bottles, rather than being ground up and turned into something other than a bottle, were sent back to bottling plants, cleaned and refilled with the appropriate liquid. It was always interesting to see how beat-up the Coca Cola bottle was after I dropped a dime into the vending machine.

There were several methods of bottle treasure hunting. Wandering through alleys, along streets, in parks and parking lots usually resulted in a bag or box overflowing with bottles. The most plentiful supply was in the gutters along main thoroughfares. There was a lot of drinking and driving back then, resulting in many bottles being thrown out or dumped along the road. I was both confused and grateful that people threw away these bottles. Why would anyone throw away money?

One of the best methods for acquiring this see-through brown, green and clear treasure was to knock on a door and ask, "Do you have any pop or beer bottles that you don't want?" Often the person asked would respond with a smile and then disappear for a minute or two and return with several bottles. It was that easy. I was saving them the bother of returning the bottles and they were providing me with the means to purchase some very necessary child provisions.

Beer bottles were worth a penny each and soda bottles two cents. That is not much, but an hour of searching could easily yield 25 to 50 cents. Back then that was a sizable amount of pocket change for a kid. Heckel's Thriftway, located two blocks from my house, was always willing to take in all the bottles I could carry. This was probably because Mr. Heckel knew all of the money he gave me would be handed back to him a few minutes later when I'd gathered all of the penny candy needed to sustain me until the next treasure hunt.

One block east of the Thriftway store was a laundromat containing three rows of coin-operated washing machines and one row of huge dryers. The point of this story is how I made some money, but in case you are curious, yes, on one occasion I did climb into a dryer and take a couple of spins.

Most everyone has experienced the task of taking laundry to a laundromat. You unload the car, place the basket of dirty clothes on the floor in front of the washer, toss in the laundry and then reach into your pocket for nickels, dimes and quarters. This is where the treasure starts unintentionally being buried. Sometimes the patron doesn't quite hit the mark when dropping the coins into the appropriate slot. The coin falls to the floor so the patron picks up the coin and tries again. Or, if my luck is good, the coins end up between, behind or under the washing machine or dryer. The washee attempts and, hopefully, fails to retrieve the coins. Eureka! The treasure has been buried. I was able to dig up the treasure by having kid-sized hands and skinny arms.

A visit to the laundromat was a regular stop on my neighborhood exploration. It was best to find a time when the fewest patrons were present so my actions would raise as little concern as possible. I'd first peek between the machines to see if any shiny coins were visible. Upon finding evidence of future fortune the money manipulating maneuvers would begin. A little wiggle here, a little push there, a hand and arm squeezed between or under machines and eventually my fingertips would be touching the entry fee to candy-land. On a good day my pockets would sing the song played by several silver coins bouncing in rhythm together.

Cracks and crevasses containing cash

There were a few short-term cash generating opportunities for Tacoma's young entrepreneur other than scrounging for castoff bottles or digging for lost coins. These opportunities included picking berries, lawn care and, in my particular case, being the neighborhood tailor and garment artist.

The city of Puyallup, located just southeast of Tacoma, was a rural community surrounded by farms where various fruits and vegetables were grown and harvested. These edibles had one main thing in common; they needed to be picked or pulled, then packed. The picking requirement was often fulfilled by children and teenagers eager to make a few dollars removing numerous species of berries off the vines. There were only two skills necessary for picking berries: don't get too scratched up while picking, and don't eat the future income.

The job began when kids of various sizes and ages gathered early in the morning at different sites around town. A dilapidated bus (usually a former school bus) would arrive to transport the sleepy little pickers. Everybody climbed into the bus, settled in for the short ride, and talked to their picking pals about what they were going to do with the money earned that day. If it was the first time picking, then the young laborer was usually confident that the work would be easy and the pay plentiful. More experienced pickers were no longer that naive.

The bus would arrive at the berry field; the occupants would disembark and then wait for instructions. Frequently these instructions came from someone who seemed to have previously been either a drill sergeant or a prison guard. Their method of communication was rarely pleasant.

"Take these boxes and fill them up with berries. When a flat is full bring it back to me and I'll record how much you picked. You'll get paid at the end of the day. Now get moving and get busy!"

A "flat" was a flat wooden box about one foot by one-and-a-half feet that contained approximately a dozen smaller wooden containers. As the berries were picked they were dropped into these smaller boxes until all of them were filled. Then the flat was taken to the former prison guard and traded for an empty flat. The goal was to fill and return as many flats as possible for as long as possible and then, hopefully, get paid a sizeable amount at the end of the day. At least that is what the pickers expected. There were, however, a few reasons why you have never known any wealthy berry pickers.

The work itself was labor intensive, especially when working on hot days. Picking a berry and dropping it into a box over and over was a tedious task and difficult to maintain. Worst of all was the various temptations surrounding you. For example, the berries were sometimes too tempting to resist. Picking a berry and dropping it into the box was often followed by picking a berry and dropping it into your mouth. It seemed like free food but actually it was stealing from the farmer and eating your income.

Another problem was the co-workers, generally categorized into three types. The first, and best, were friends who joined you on your quest for cash. Working with them might provide positive motivation, or negative distraction. Talking and picking was fine but too much talking usually resulted in too little picking and too little income. It might also cause the prison guard to scold you as if you were part of a Louisiana chain-gang.

The second picking type was the local kid who wanted you to know he was not impressed that you came from the big city of Tacoma. Tacoma was not anything close to being a "Big City," but there always seemed to be at least one farmer's bulky teenage son who wanted to challenge the slickers from the city. I witnessed a few minor fights but, fortunately, I was never one of the participants who was rolling around in the dirt and squished berries.

The third type of picker was by far the most dangerous. They were girls! My berry picking summers were during the period of my life when most boys suddenly begin taking notice of girls. It's a mystery how it happens, but suddenly the females of approximately the same age, many that you've known your entire life, have changed from being tolerated to being temptresses. A good example was Patty who lived on my block. For years she was just someone taking up space in my world. Then, unexpectedly, Patty became someone that I could not stop taking notice of. When did she get so pretty, and when did she stop looking like a boy wearing a dress? Why was it that for years I didn't care one way or another if she knew I existed; then, mysteriously, I wanted to make sure she noticed that I was noticing her?

So there I'd be on a hot and dusty summer day picking berries when I'd look over the bush and see a girl I'd never met before smile at me and, for some unknown reason, it would make me turn a color resembling the raspberries that I was picking.

"Hi. Um, er, where, um, where do you go to school?" I'd ask.

If I was lucky the parallel picker would give me a little of her time. Even if she chose not to converse with me, I still gained from the exchange a bit more experience in connecting with the newly appreciated other half of the human race.

At the end of the day I'd receive my pay of a few dollars, take a last glance at the girl I met earlier, then ride the bus back home and give thought to other possible ways of making money.

Picking up various odd jobs around the neighborhood was another source of income. The crabby guy across the alley hired me to weed his yard. This was the same yard that he'd yell at me to stop running across on my journey to the home of the previously referenced and now fascinating neighbor girl Patty. I'd weed, he'd inspect my work and grumble his approval, then hand me a dollar or two.

There was a duplex one block away, and the owner paid very well for just watering his lawn. All that was required was a daily dousing, which I made even more interesting by turning the patio area and nearby steps into a multiple level waterfall. It was fun to spray my friends as they passed by or stopped for a visit. I think I was fired from that job.

My tailoring career also began in the neighborhood. There was a popular fad in the late 1950s and early 1960s of wearing blue jeans, preferably Levis brand, that had been "pegged." Pegging consisted of re-sewing the pants legs so they were very tight around the wearer's legs. If the pants were nearly impossible to both put on and take off, then the "pegging" had been done perfectly.

From a very early age I was fascinated with my mother's sewing machine—fascinated enough that I learned how to operate it. I became proficient enough to successfully peg a pair of my own pants and, as a result, word spread quickly through the neighborhood and I became a professional pants pegger. For the sum of fifty cents, customers could strut around town with what appeared to be denim spray-painted on their lower torso and legs. It was a short-lived career, since the number of neighborhood parents allowing their offspring to wear pegged pants was limited and the demand quickly ended. Pegged pants were associated with hoodlums and young people who were destined for a life of crime. This proved to be true for a couple of my customers.

Another fad during the pegged pants era was wearing "monster shirts." These were T-shirts and sweatshirts with cartoon characters drawn on the front using felt pens and spray paint. The monster reference is because the characters, rather than being popular comic-strip stars of the day, or cute Disney type animals, were grotesque monsters with giant teeth and drooling tongues. These creatures were always driving outrageous hot rods. Ed "Big Daddy" Roth was the best known monster shirt artist in the world, and his two best known characters were a slathering and bulging eyed rat known as "Rat Fink" and a strange and unidentifiable creature known as "Mother's Worry."

I had just enough talent with pen and paint to draw a reasonable copy of both creatures. The result of this talent

and willingness to plagiarize Ed Roth was acquiring 50 cents from any kid who brought me his soon-to-be-parentally-disapproved garment. As with the pegged pants, the market demand quickly dried up and I had to move on to another source of income.

I had the good fortune to meet Ed Roth a few decades later and shared with him my history of plagiarizing his work. Ed, a very large man, placed his monster sized artistic hand on my shoulder, leaned over, looked me directly in the eyes and said, "Well son, I guess you owe me some money." Fortunately his comment was followed by a hearty laugh.

The "kid" time in my life began fading away and the need for something resembling a real job became more important. My teenage years began with "boy" jobs: paperboy delivering newspapers, busboy working in a restaurant, box boy working in a grocery store. These were followed by other real jobs that earned me the income I needed. But as I look back, none of these held quite the enjoyment of knocking on doors, finding treasure, discovering girls or being the neighborhood pegger/painter.

Subterranean Secrets

The house I grew up in had several special places. Like many homes built in the 1920s, it had an attic that seemed mysterious, a little creepy, and within the various boxes and containers stored were cherished memories and a few useless items from the past. The closets in our bedrooms were large and provided good hiding places. The kitchen had a breakfast nook that looked just like a booth in a restaurant. The dining room had leaded glass cabinets that displayed our better dishes and glassware. But best of all was the basement.

Most of the houses in the neighborhood had basements, but my opinion was that none of them were as good as our basement. My friend Dale's basement was small and dirty because of the coal that was stored for the furnace, although it was almost fun to help him shovel the black lumps into the furnace's flames. Jacky's basement was just a dungeon packed full of boxes. Dan's parents tried to make their basement look like a bar frequented by Polynesians and, as they reminded us frequently, anywhere below the first floor was off limits to Dan and any of his friends.

The basement in our home was a place of wonder as I was growing up. Entering this subterranean world exposed me to visual delights, dangerous items, creative opportunities, magical contraptions, threats from enemy governments and numerous secrets waiting to be discovered.

At the bottom of the stairs against the opposite wall sat the washer and dryer. They were matching Westinghouse washing machine and dryer models that were very distinctive in design and marketed with the sales pitch, "America's Favorite Laundry Twins." Perhaps the reason that I'm able to remember them is because the access doors for the clothes, at least to my eyes, resembled the front of an automobile. Both of these porcelain covered, front loading appliances provided me with hours of entertainment.

On laundry days my mother would load up the washer and then, when the wash cycle was completed, transfer the wet laundry to the dryer. Both the washer and dryer had a glass window in the door that resembled a large porthole. The clothes were visible as they sloshed in the soapy water and tumbled in the dryer. I loved to sit on the bottom stairstep and watch the washer as it did its dirty duty and then the dryer as it changed my soggy socks into hot hosiery. To my eyes each tumble was like a snowflake—different than the last tumble and never to be duplicated.

On cold days the dryer provided the perfect amount of heat. The appliance was designed in a way that the bottom slanted back towards the top at just the right angle for me to lean against it to warm my body. Sitting on top of the dryer and hanging my legs over the front also provided an excellent source of warm comfort.

The dryer provided another bit of magic: lint. To me, the lint trap was like a Las Vegas slot machine. The more clothes in the dryer, the bigger the prize. I would carefully peel the layer of lint from the screen and look closely to see if I could recognize the tiny particles and identify which towel, rag or article of clothing these nearly microscopic specks had once been a part of. Then I'd do some simple thing like try to spread out the lint layer without breaking it apart, or try to compress it into a little fuzzy ball. The more lint the better, and something like a blanket being put into the dryer would be a bonanza to me.

As I write this story it is 60 years later and I have a front loading washer with a glass door. Yes, I still often find myself taking a moment or two to watch the clothes tumble and the suds splash. There is no window on the dryer door, but there is a lint trap and, yes, I often can't resist peeling and playing with the fuzzy layer.

Just to the right of my childhood home's basement stairs was my father's workshop, with the expected workbench and array of tools. There were also several shelves lined with bottles containing screws, nails and various metal things that might be useful in a future project or repair job. But there were two tools in the workshop that I found especially fascinating.

The more exciting of the two was a magical maker of sparks. This handheld gizmo was used to start the flame on a small tank of butane. The flame was then used for various jobs such as melting lead on plumbing fittings or soldering wires. The spark maker (that's what I always called it) was operated by squeezing a thick U-shaped wire that had a rough surface on one side and a cigarette lighter flint on the other. Sparks were created as these surfaces made contact, and to me it looked like a 4th-of-July sparkler. I played with it repeatedly until the flints were worn down. Dad never complained about my overuse, and new flints always magically appeared.

The second tool, and one that still fascinates me today, was the vise. This powerful tool looked to me like a medieval torture device, and it certainly inflicted severe pain on many tin cans, scraps of metal and pieces of wood. A malfunctioning pocket-sized transistor radio screamed out in agony as it was compressed into a splintered clump of plastic bits and unrepairable Japanese technology. Empty beer cans were reduced to lumpy discs suitable for skipping across the basement floor. Occasionally I tested my ability to withstand pain by placing a finger into the vise, turning the handle and seeing how much pressure the evil torturer (me) could administer to the poor prisoner (me) before all top-secret information was revealed.

Watching my big brother repair motorcycle and car parts in the workshop was interesting, and his rebuilding of a Matchless motorcycle in the basement provided me with the opportunity to expand my understanding of things mechanical and also learn what methods of repair work can't be done safely inside the basement.

There was also one item in Dad's workshop that proved to be a sort of IQ test for me. The item was a flare gun. Most flare guns are basically a pistol with a large diameter barrel; however, the one in the workshop 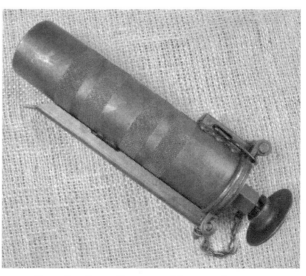 was just a tube about five inches long with a plunger type firing pin on one end. You operated it by simply unscrewing the plunger end, inserting a shotgun-shell-sized flare and screwing the plunger end back on. Then, when your ship was sinking, or bears were attacking, or you were sitting on your upside-down car at the bottom of a ravine, you aimed the tube skyward, pulled the plunger, released, and boom, a ball of fire sped into the sky. According to the movies I'd seen, rescuers arrived very soon after spotting the fireball on the horizon.

This is what the part of my brain with an average I.Q. already knew. But the other part—the one with an I.Q. below 50—was curious about another possible use for the flare gun. The flare, as mentioned, looked just like a shotgun shell and appeared to be the same size.

My father, being a police officer, had a variety of interesting things, including firearms and ammunition, in his basement office (I'll get to this room later). Amongst the items in the office was a desk drawer containing a box of shotgun shells. My inferior-IQ brain decided to find out if a shotgun shell was, in fact, the same size as a flare. From out of dad's drawer a shell came and into the flare gun it went. It fit perfectly. Now what do I do with this discovery?

Every red-blooded boy knows anything that goes boom, makes fire and puts holes in things is desirable. My inferior-IQ brain was sure that the flare gun in my hand was capable of doing all three of these things, but for some reason I was hesitant to find out. This tube with a plunger on one end was designed to safely shoot a flare towards the ozone layer, so why would it not safely do the same when loaded with a shotgun shell? While facing the concrete wall I firmly held the tube with my left hand, grasped the plunger handle between the fingers of my right hand and began to pull. Fortunately my average-IQ brain was active enough to feel a slight sense of danger. I might even have had a fleeting thought that I was about to do something that I'd very much regret. I decided to remove the shotgun shell and replace it with the proper projectile.

Looking back on this incident makes me wonder what would have happened, had I not removed the shotgun shell. Maybe I wouldn't have enough fingers to be dancing around the keyboard in front of me.

The flare gun did finally get used, but not for my personal rescue from some disaster. The University of Puget Sound (College of Puget Sound when I was a kid) had a large gymnasium, known as the Field House, located a short distance from my home. There was a large parking lot next to the building that seemed like a safe place, due to its size, to try out the flare gun and not do any harm to myself or anyone else. Well, that is what I intended. Late one evening I walked to the parking lot, pointed the flare gun towards the sky and pulled the plunger. The flare shot upwards beautifully, gracefully arched towards the gymnasium and plummeted earthward until it landed on the roof of the building. Then a small fire began on the roof. I quickly left the area and, fortunately, did not hear any sirens that night or read any stories the next day about a fire at the Field House. I continued to play with the flare gun but never again loaded it with either a flare or a shotgun shell.

Just outside the workshop door was another item that kept me mesmerized for years. There was a large wooden structural beam extending the length of the ceiling just below the kitchen and bathroom floors that were above on the first floor. From this beam there was something hanging that was fascinating and beautiful: a perfectly formed drip of what appeared to be sap from the wood beam. It was large, long, transparent and amber in color. Over a period of several years I would stand below it or sit on the basement stairs and admire how perfectly it was formed. After a few years I decided that a closer look was warranted. I had grown enough to be able to maneuver a ladder so that I could climb up to take a closer look. I was in for a surprise.

There was a reason the long and large drop of sap was so perfect. It was not sap leaking from the beam. Instead, it was a piece of glass that had likely been part of a lamp or chandelier. Instead of leaking from the beam, it was held in place by a very small nail. I was let down upon realizing that this thing of beauty was not a natural phenomena, but pleased that the "sap" could be removed and admired closely whenever I so desired. It continued to hold my fascination for many years.

At the opposite end of the room housing the glass sap was the furnace. Behind the furnace was a secret room that only I knew about, or at least that is what I believed.

A popular television show for a few years during my childhood was called *I Led Three Lives*. From October of 1953 until the end of 1955 actor Richard Carlson played the part of an advertising executive who had infiltrated the United States Communist Party on behalf of the Federal Bureau of Investigation. Herbert Philbrick, played by Carlson, had a

secret room in his basement. He would sneak into this room, sit at his desk and write reports on the activities of the local chapter of the Communist Party. I wondered, after watching a few episodes of the show, if there was also a secret room in the Lambert basement. It was certainly worth searching for and, much to my excitement, I found an area good enough to consider my "secret room" search a complete success.

The furnace was installed at an angle in the corner of one area of the basement. There was just enough room on one side of the furnace for my young body (6 years old when *I Led Three Lives* began) to squeeze through. Much to my delight, behind the furnace there was a triangle shaped area large enough for me to sit and pretend that I too was working for the FBI. A bonus was that I could hide from my family and the rest of the world

whenever I was tucked away in the furnace fortress writing imaginary reports. No doubt several no-good, stinking, pinko Commies were exposed as a result of my clandestine solitary activity behind the oil burning furnace secret passageway.

My father's "office" was the best place in the basement. In it he had a desk and chair, a military surplus metal framed single bed and a couple of old wooden chairs. In the corner was a partially completed closet that provided access to the dirt-floored crawlspace located under the front portion of our house. The desk in the office was the source of many delights that ranged from it operating like a Chinese-puzzle-box to it containing some highly dangerous and highly educational items.

The desk had a built-in trapdoor system that allowed a typewriter to magically appear by lifting and pushing a handle at the front of the desk. As it was pushed a portion of the desk's top went up, back and then mysteriously dropped down into the back. At the same time, another portion of the desk raised up to replace the now absent top. The bonus was that the replacement had a typewriter sitting on it. This, to my young eyes and mind, was absolutely magic beyond belief. I would wrestle that top up and over and back again repeatedly to see the typewriter appear, disappear and then reappear. I understood how it worked but still marveled at the engineering that was needed to make this magic happen.

**Chinese
puzzle
desk**

Another part of the Chinese-puzzle-box desk was the magic drawers. There was a sequence that had to be followed in order to get any drawer open. If the top drawer was to be opened, the bottom drawer first had to be opened a couple of inches, then the top drawer could be opened. If the middle drawer was to be opened, the bottom was opened a little, then the top a little, then the middle could be opened all the way. I don't know if the desk was designed this way or if there was some internal malfunction in the locking system but, whatever the reason, it was fun solving the drawer puzzle.

The question might be asked as to what was I doing in my father's office and going through his desk? A question that I had but never verbalized was why didn't he ever ask, "Who has been going through my desk?" It certainly was a good question, since my rummaging through his drawers revealed a pistol, switchblade knife, brass knuckles and a billy club. Also discovered were educational materials that assisted my entrance into young adulthood and answered some questions I had about the opposite sex. These items also created a few new questions that were not answered for many years.

Dad's office also was used as a meeting place for fellow members of the Oddballs. This short-lived club consisted of me and a few friends from the neighborhood. It was organized enough that the name of the club was written in pencil on the exterior surface of the outside basement entry door. I recall one meeting consisting of sitting on the surplus military bed and reading copies of *Dennis the Menace* and *Beetle Bailey* comic books.

Dad's office also provided the location for one of the most important decisions of my life. I wish more of my friends had made the same decision.

Smoking cigarettes was common in the 1950s and 1960s. Experimenting with tobacco seemed to start around 12 years of age, and my friends and I were right on schedule. My father smoked in his office, so it provided the perfect place to try puffing a pack with my friends and not needing to worry about the telltale smell.

I remember sitting with three or four friends as we passed a pack of cigarettes amongst us. They were sitting on the surplus bed while I sat at my dad's desk. This was not the first time we'd smoked together and, for a couple of the guys, this was the beginning of a lifetime of smoking. As I was leaning back in my father's chair and watching them puff away, a few thoughts were running through my mind. A pack of cigarettes at that time cost twenty-five cents. Most of the smokers I knew (mostly our fathers) were one pack to three packs-a-day smokers. The cost of a single pack-a-day multiplied times 365 days equaled $91.25. Back then that amount of money could pay for an excellent quality record player. I had neither a poor quality nor an excellent quality record player. I did not have any record player. The solution seemed obvious: if I saved 25 cents a day instead of spending it on cigarettes, I'd soon have enough money to buy a record player. I made the decision at that moment. At the same time I formed the opinion that anyone who smoked was crazy. My plan worked perfectly, and I saved enough cigarette money to buy a good record player.

As I grew older I no longer could squeeze behind the furnace. My dad had moved out of the house and his office became just a storage area. Staring at the washer and dryer didn't seem like a good way to spend my time. Basements, however, still fascinate me today. I occasionally stop at estate sales and real estate open houses and head to the basement as quickly as possible in the hope of discovering someone else's memories.

Judy and Jack

Everyone is familiar with *The Tonight Show* and most of the hosts over the nearly 65 years that it has been broadcast on television. The current host, Jimmy Fallon, was preceded by Jay Leno, Conan O'Brien, Johnny Carson, Jack Paar, Steve Allen and, briefly, Ernie Kovacs, Jack Lescoulie and Al Collins. They all had their good points, but I like Jack Paar the best because my sister Judy and I used to hang out with him.

When I was a young boy I considered my sister to be worldly and sophisticated. This opinion was perhaps due to her being seven years older than me and, therefore, sometimes seeming more like an adult living in our house rather than a sibling vying for our parents' attention. She did things like poke holes in her ears to hang things from, willingly ironed her clothes, sang without being embarrassed and attended church even when she didn't have to. These were certainly the actions of an adult and not anything that I would do voluntarily. To this day I still do not have a hole in either of my ears, and I continue to not iron any of my clothes.

I don't recall ever harassing or cruelly teasing Judy and, instead, spent most of my time with her seeking approval and guidance. Often, I'd go to her with a question or concern before I'd go to my parents.

When my cousin Linda broke a dish and I was blamed for it, I decided to run away from home. I took a small suitcase from my sister's room and packed it with everything needed by a 7-year-old boy leaving home forever. The suitcase was made to carry her Betsy Wetsy doll and doll clothes, so it was just big enough to carry a couple pairs of underpants and a T-shirt. I was sure this was all that was needed for my new life on the road.

Judy came into my room, saw Miss Wetsy's suitcase and asked me, "What are you doing?"

I expressed the injustice suffered when the dish that had been broken by my evil cousin was blamed on me, and that I'd teach my parents a lesson by walking out the door, never to return. No doubt I'd be quickly adopted by a very rich and loving couple who would supply me with truckloads of dishes that I could break whenever I felt the desire. I might even let my parents know where I lived so they could stand outside the gated estate and watch me riding to and fro (whatever that means) on horseback while flinging dishes hither and yon (another whatever).

My sister, being 14 years old at the time and, therefore, overflowing with wisdom, expressed her opinion that perhaps I was overreacting to the dish incident and that a stray little boy being adopted by a wealthy couple with a lot of extra dishes was likely a rare occurrence. I listened to her intently, looked out my bedroom window at the gathering clouds in the sky, and then opened Betsy Wetsy's suitcase. I removed the survival gear and handed the suitcase back to Judy. I think the depression and frustration from the destroyed dish injustice lasted for at least another 20 minutes, after which my cousin Linda and I probably settled the score by playing a game of checkers or Go Fish.

My big sister was occasionally given the duty of watching over the safety of my brother Lynn and me. He and I were good at entertaining ourselves, so her only real requirements were to listen for any screams resulting from one of us falling out of our bedroom windows, setting fire to ourselves in the back yard or any other life-threatening activities. She would engage in whatever activity she preferred, such as doing homework, while Lynn and I engaged in our activity of choice, which never included doing homework. Rarely did her duties require anything more than making sure we were fed and in bed at the appointed time.

This story began with a short history of *The Tonight* Show and a comment about hanging out with Jack Paar. That's because my most cherished memories of time spent with Judy also included Jack.

The show came on late at night, especially for a little brother still

in grade school. My bedtime was 8 or 9 p.m., and Jack appeared on our giant Zenith black & white television at 10 or 11 p.m., well past when Judy should have sent me upstairs to brush my teeth, put on my pajamas, say my prayers (God bless Mommy, Daddy, Judy, Lynn, Grandma and Grandpa, Doug and Juanita, Cindy and Linda, Hi and Alice, Ricky, Darrell and Dennis) and climb into bed. On very special occasions she altered this routine by letting me stay up late with her and watch Jack Paar at his desk on the set of *The Tonight Show.*

Sophistication has been a theme thus far and there was another example of it on these special big sister & little brother nights.

Back then everyone I knew was of the opinion that serving cheese on a cracker was a sign of good taste, both of the combination being served and of the host doing the serving. I was delighted when Judy asked if I wanted to stay up late and watch Jack with her. This usually happened when

Mom and Dad were out late, or perhaps when they had gone to bed early, or Dad was doing a late shift in his job as a police officer. I don't recall my brother participating in any of these late night viewings. I probably felt that he was not quite sophisticated enough.

Judy would go to the kitchen and gather up the necessary items for our late night pleasure. The cheese was always Velveeta and the crackers were always Saltines. These delicacies were artistically arranged on a plate and served with all the grace and style that only a 15-year-old girl could master. The slices of Velveeta would be cut into perfect squares and placed on each individual Saltine cracker. The plate placed before me appeared worthy of being served at any White House dinner or star-studded Hollywood affair.

There on the coffee table would be the waiting gourmet delight, on the television screen would be the smartest and funniest guy I'd ever seen, and alongside me was my sophisticated big sister making sure I had all the cheese and crackers needed to keep my body nourished while Jack Paar nourished my young brain.

Jack would say goodnight to both of us and Judy and I would say goodnight to each other. In a short time I'd be snuggled in bed feeling a little smarter thanks to Jack, and a little more sophisticated and secure thanks to Judy.

Jack Paar

Judy continued being a wonderful sister and helped me through a few tough times. One day she took me for a walk and let me know that Mom and Dad were getting a divorce. She did it in a way that convinced me this was a good thing for the family and not a tragedy. She taught me that a gentleman always walks on the curbside of a lady. She gave me driving lessons in her 1952 Oldsmobile and never yelled at me. Her shoulder soaked up a few of my tears when my high school sweetheart broke up with me. Her advice helped me deal with a few disagreements with my parents.

She continued helping others throughout her life. There are hundreds of adults who look back to their school days and consider her one of their favorite teachers. Her church was blessed with her labors and her voice. Her sons were guided by her beliefs and her friends were helped in their times of need.

Judy passed away a few years ago. I had the honor of being there and holding her hand when she took her last breath. The only thing missing in the room was a plate of Velveeta cheese and Saltine crackers.

Squirts in the Cockpit

A good friend when I was growing up was my buddy Greg Eling. We were car crazy kids that spent a lot of time together learning about cars and deciding what we would be driving in the future. In the meantime we decided to become airplane pilots.

Oswald Field was located near the west edge of town. It was a small airport that was home to numerous small aircraft flown by private pilots. Located there was also a small charter airline company that stored its single and double engine planes in a large hanger.

The year was 1957 and Greg and I were just a couple of little squirts. Greg's family had recently moved near Oswald Field, providing us with a new and exotic place to be a couple of nuisances. Our mothers would pack us sack lunches and we'd walk the short distance to the airfield. We'd stroll around the field admiring various airplanes, watch them taking off and landing, snoop into the hangers, and just soak up the sounds and smells of a small community airfield.

Did we ever get to take a flight in any aircraft? Well, sort of, but not before we had the proper nourishment.

The Airport Café was located across the street from the airport. Greg and I would take our sack lunches into the restaurant and sit at the counter. There we'd order a glass of water and then drop in the Fizzies tablets that were included with our lunch. Some readers may remember these little colored tablets. They were basically fruit flavored Alka-Seltzer tablets ("Plop plop, fizz fizz, oh what a relief it is!") that, when dropped into a glass of water, turned into a very poor substitute for a glass of soda pop.

Greg and Lance waiting for their next flight

It was very nervy to sit at a restaurant eating food that you brought yourself, and then order a glass of water, however, the waitresses behind the counter seemed to love it. We were just a couple of cute little boys that likely brought out the mothering instincts in these gracious ladies. On at least one occasion they brought us, at no charge, a large plate of French fries to enjoy along with our peanut butter and jelly sandwiches.

We'd finish our lunches and then return to the field and get ready to pilot our own aircraft.

There was a large gully a short distance from the landing strip. This gully provided a dumping spot for every unwanted piece of broken machinery, metal refuse or anything else that was deemed to be worthless. It was also the location of a very broken airplane.

An abandoned cockpit similar to the one used by Greg and Lance

There before us sat the carcass of what used to be a twin-engine airplane. My guess is that it was either an Apache or a Cessna, or something similar. Or, perhaps, I wanted it to be that type of aircraft since a Cessna T-50 was what one of my television heroes piloted every week on the *Sky King* show. Regardless of what it actually was, there was enough left for two young imaginary pilots to fly into the wild blue yonder. It looked like the skeleton of an aircraft with a few pieces of "flesh" left in place. Greg and I would sit in what

Greg and Lance reminiscing about their days at Oswald field

remained of the cockpit and take turns being the pilot and co-pilot. Dozens of enemy aircraft were sent spiraling to the ground in flames, victims of our keen fighter pilot skills. Hundreds of happy passengers were flown to their destinations safely thanks to the navigational abilities of the two young gentlemen in the cockpit.

I do not know the history of this forlorn piece of flying machinery that was abandoned in the gully. We decided it was pushed there after a crash landing, but it was more likely just a worn out aircraft that had served its purpose and now provided spare parts for adult pilots and fantasy flights for young pilots.

As we grew older the trips to the airport were replaced with other activities. The passion for automobiles continued growing and eventually we were both piloting our own cars.

Greg and I have remained good friends and occasionally reminisce about our Oswald adventures. A strip mall and Tacoma Community College now stand where we once fought our WWII dogfights in the skies over Germany. Greg's current fighter is a hot rod 1936 Chevrolet coupe. My squadron includes a 1950 Studebaker with the famous "Bulletnose" in the front, making it resemble the front of a Lockheed P-38 Fighter.

I guess I'm still the little kid that liked to hang around at Oswald Field.

Sorry George

Almost every boy and girl I grew up with was a scout of some sort: Cub, Brownie, Campfire, Boy, Girl, whatever. "Scouting" was what a kid in my neighborhood did, and I was no different. Every week I put on my blue shirt and yellow bandanna and went to George Marco's house for our "Den Meeting." The meetings were fun and came with two bonuses: treats and George's mother.

We opened the meeting by pledging allegiance to the flag and doing the two-finger salute while reciting what good young men we promised to be; then there was a special activity. We learned important skills, such as how to burn our initials into a piece of scrap wood, how to tie various rope knots that we would never use in our entire lives, and how to punch holes in jar lids so bugs could breathe.

I didn't mind all of this nearly mindless activity because, as I said above, George's mom was there. Mrs. Marco was perhaps the most beautiful woman that I'd ever seen. Even at my very young age I had an appreciation for female beauty, and Mrs. Marco had busloads of it. Granted, she was really old, probably at least 35, but I didn't care because to gaze upon her face was to gaze upon Webster's definition of beauty. She was Donna Reed, Loretta Young and Grace Kelly combined. No, she was even prettier than that to this 10-year-old Cub Scout.

My participation at the meetings consisted of fumbling with the evening's project while keeping my eyes locked on

Mrs. Marco. I didn't care that I ended up with glue all over my shirt or that my initialed piece of wood was smoldering into ashes. I was only there to look at my beautiful Den Mother. Mother nothing; this was the older woman of my young dreams.

I realized that it was not acceptable for me to have these feelings. In fact any Cub Scout who had any interest in creepy girls, or women, obviously had a problem. Females were only supposed to become tolerable when you had a few years of Boy Scouting under your handmade belt. Cub Scouts thought that girls had cooties and belonged anywhere other than where the Cub Scouts belonged. Brownie or Campfire Girls meeting in a far-away basement or school gym were where they belonged. But Mrs. Marco was the exception. Unfortunately I couldn't keep my feelings to myself.

One of Lance's last days in uniform

My Cub Scout Den was asked to perform the flag salute ceremony and lead the Pledge of Allegiance at the local Daughters of the American Revolution meeting. This was quite an honor in our minds, and we wanted to do a good job for these women that, much to my confusion, could not possibly be the actual daughters of anyone who fought in the Revolutionary War. We practiced the ceremony and prepared for our big night. I wanted to do an excellent job, not because I cared about the ceremony, but because Mrs. Marco might smile in my direction and nod her approval. Maybe she'd even pat me on the shoulder or muss my hair after the ceremony. These possible rewards were not going to happen; instead, my membership in Cub Scouts was about to voluntarily expire, and my relationship with George Marco was about to end.

The D.A.R. meeting was about to start and we were getting ready to begin the ceremony. As the white-gloved and finely coiffed ladies rose to their feet I, for some unknown and soon-to-be-regretted reason, leaned over to George and said, "I think you mother is pretty." George, curse his evil soul, then leaned over to his mother, my Den Mother and the prettiest woman in the history of women, and told her what I had said. She chuckled and I turned bright red. My face was likely redder than the red on Old Glory. And the red on the outside was matched by a red-alert level of humiliation on the inside.

Looking back on the incident, I don't know why I was so humiliated and embarrassed. I suppose it was because I was 10 years old and not equipped with the maturity necessary to know that it might be good for Mrs. Marco to know my feelings. If she knew of my adoration, I might get a bit more attention from her and perhaps an extra cookie or two at the end of our weekly Den meetings.

None of these possibilities came to mind. All I knew was that George had ruined my life. How could I face Mrs. Marco again? Would George think I was weird because I thought his mother was pretty? Would the other Cubs ridicule me for liking a creepy female? I was not going to stick around to find out.

I don't recall how the rest of the evening went, either because I have blocked it out of my mind or I blacked out during the ceremony. I never went to another Den meeting for fear that something bad would happen. Of course I wanted attention from Mrs. Marco, but would it result in me being ridiculed, throwing up, wetting my pants or all three? Would a smile on her lips and a touch of my shoulder result in me suddenly sprouting a mustache and my voice sounding like James Earl Jones? It seemed to me that the best way to handle the situation was to never go to another den meeting. It seemed like a good decision at the time.

Perhaps Mrs. Marco now resides in the big Cub Scout Den in the sky and George has no memory of me or the incident. Maybe I was not alone in my opinion of Mrs. Marco. Maybe nobody made the connection as to why I didn't return to the meetings. I don't know for sure because I never spoke to George Marco again. Over the next few years I matured enough to know that I'd been terribly unfair to George, but by then it was too late. My embarrassment over telling George that I thought his mother was pretty was replaced by embarrassment that I'd handled the situation badly and had overreacted a bit to George sharing my secret with his mother.

Sorry George.

Spoiled Victory

I have no big regrets in my life. I do, however, have several small ones, including a day at school when I "won" a prize.

The grade school I attended, Tacoma's Franklin Elementary School, had a "Cleanup Contest" every year. The teachers gave the students burlap bags and sent them out to clean up the school grounds. The student returning with the most garbage won a prize.

The front of Franklin Elementary School

I was in fifth grade the year that I was the winner. The prize was an ice cream bar (vanilla ice cream covered with chocolate) that you got to eat during class without getting into trouble. I still remember the guilt I felt while consuming it in front of admiring classmates.

At the start of the event, the students gathered in the playground and waited for the bags to be distributed. While waiting I looked around to develop a winning strategy that would result in my bag being the fullest. We were allowed to step outside of the fence surrounding the playground to search for refuse on the outer perimeter of the school property. This, I reasoned, would likely be the most lucrative place to locate a winning supply of garbage and result in the ice cream bar finding its way to my stomach.

My first move was a smart one: going directly to the farthest corner of the school grounds. The other students started looking for trash in the schoolyard along with a couple hundred other students looking in the same place. I, shrewdly, went where no one else thought to venture. This choice was sure to result in a burlap bag brimming with garbage.

I walked along the fence and began filling the bag with gooey candy wrappers, crumpled lunch bags, dirt covered apple cores, discarded school papers and other items that grade school kids didn't bother to throw into the trash. The bag was slowly filling but was not yet full to a winning load when I spotted a stash of garbage that would surely result in the coveted ice cream bar being awarded to me. There was one problem, however; the garbage was not on the school's property.

The area I was searching abutted an alley. Across the alley was an old dilapidated garage filled with the appropriate refuse. This was not a typical garage filled with old car parts and broken down furniture. It was, instead, full of crumpled papers, water-stained boxes, food wrappers and other castoffs that would surely convince the teachers that these items had previously been drifting across the schoolyard like tumbleweeds in an old western movie.

I had a choice to make: continue poking around the school property looking for a gum wrapper here and an orange peel there, or walk across the alley and assure myself of Cleanup Contest conquest!

Playground area behind Franklin Elementary School

I made a poor choice that still haunts me to this day.

Into the garage I went to select the appropriate pieces of garbage to place in the bag. In a short time the bag was brimming, as was my smile, and I returned to the schoolyard and turned in my bag for contest winning consideration. The teachers complimented me on the successful search, classmates looked upon the cache with envy and I returned to the classroom confident that after school my mother would ask how I got a chocolate stain on my shirt.

The moment arrived for the winning student to be notified and awarded the soon-to-be-devoured trophy. The principal came into the classroom, told everyone that I was the winner and gave me the ice cream bar. The teacher encouraged me to begin eating as my classmates watched. I began to make quick work of the coveted award.

Being the center of attention has always been one of my life's goals and also one of its curses. It was with mixed emotions that I licked the chocolate coating as the students watched. They all probably wished that they had tried just a little harder to find more garbage and didn't realize that their garbage was honorably acquired while mine was pilfered from outside of the school's property.

The teacher and students patiently waited for me to finish devouring my reward. As the bar got smaller my guilt grew larger. Did they know that I had cheated to win the contest? Someone must have seen me sneaking across the alley to toss illegal garbage into my bag. Did the teacher know that the chocolate flavor was tainted and my guilty pleasure was much more guilt than pleasure?

I finished the winning dessert and the school day was soon over. My classmates quickly forgot the glory of my victory, and we all continued carelessly throwing garbage around the school grounds.

The ice cream bar was sweet but the victory was not.

Peanut Plunge

I'm confident that Jimmy Carlson and I have done something that very few people have done.

There were a few products produced in Tacoma that made the residents proud. The Continental Bakery made Wonder Bread and other various baked products that filled the air with luscious odors that probably added inches to our waists. The Brown & Haley Company created Almond Roca candy that was unusual and delicious at the same time. The Nalley Company pumped out pickles and other vinegar-marinated products that insured successful picnics across the country. And best of all, the Rex F. Adams Company made one of the most appreciated delights in the history of the world: peanut butter.

Jimmy Carlson's dad was a traveling salesman for the Adams Company. His job was to traverse the nation and convince storeowners and managers that the Northwest's favorite peanut product should be placed at eye level on every store's sandwich ingredient shelf.

On a few occasions Jimmy and I accompanied his father to the factory. As would be expected it smelled wonderful, as the odors of peanuts and freshly made warm peanut butter wafted through the corridors. In addition, there were large pieces of machinery that looked like contraptions used in medieval times to grind wheat or fling fiery balls at approaching enemies. Amongst the various machines and bags of peanuts was something that very few people have seen and even fewer have used as a means of recreational entertainment.

Prior to the beginning of the peanut butter process the peanuts needed to be readied for de-shelling. Thousands (millions?) of unshelled peanuts were placed in a huge container that looked like a wooden hot tub that might be  found on King Kong's deck. Access to this tub was via a ladder and walkway that led to the top of the container. On one or two occasions Jimmy and I climbed up the ladder, walked along the walkway, and arrived at the spot that provided us with a view of the sea of peanuts below us. Imagine a bowl of peanuts at a party, and then in your imagination expand the view by a billion. That is what lay before us. The peanuts were dry, still in the shells and it all resembled the children's plastic ball pits found at some family restaurants.

Jimmy and I looked at each other, glanced around to see if we were being observed, and upon realizing that there was no adult supervision nearby we dove in! We thrashed about and let our grade-school-sized bodies "float" on the sea of peanuts. There was no water in the tub, just thousands of peanuts. We did our imitation of Olympic style synchronized swimming and then made peanut angels in the style of snow angels. When fatigue set in we took a break and began shelling peanuts and having a meal that would be the envy of any elephant.

In a short time Jimmy's father decided that his son and son's sidekick needed to remove themselves from the tub filled with the better half of future peanut butter and jelly sandwiches. We reluctantly retreated from the sea of shells and prepared for the return to our homes.

As I grew older, various jobs based on food came and went in my life. I served food, cleaned tables when the food was eaten, washed the dishes and cleaned the restaurants where the food was served. I was the assistant manager of a Pizza Haven and made and baked so many pizzas that I couldn't eat one for at least 10 year after I quit working there. But Mr. Carlson and Jimmy provided me with my only opportunity to swim in food!

I've had a special appreciation for Adams Peanut Butter for the past 60 years. It is excellent for both sandwiches and swimming.

Lawn and Order

We've all experienced being in the wrong place at the wrong time. When I was 10 years old I was in the right place to observe someone else being in the wrong place.

My dad was cutting the grass and I was weeding and trimming some bushes when we heard the sound of a loud exhaust emitting from a nearby car. A '40 Ford coupe then stopped at the intersection about a half block away from us and sat with the engine idling. I was excited because I had not seen the coupe in our neighborhood before and a 1940 Ford was, and still is, my favorite car from the 1940s. My father paid little attention, but I stood there mesmerized by the sight and sound of the noisy hot rod.

A short time passed and then the driver revved up the engine, let out the clutch and accelerated rapidly down the street. My father glanced up, watched the car speed past our house and then disappear down the street. I thought it was very exciting, but my father seemed uninterested.

A short time later the same thing happened. The '40 Ford stopped in the intersection, revved up the engine and again raced pass our house. This time my father watched the hot rod's entire exercise in acceleration. Dad took off his gloves, walked into the house and returned a minute or two carrying something.

My father, being a police officer, returned from work five days a week with various police officers' equipment. His uniform hung in the closet, his gun was placed into a drawer and his utility belt (handcuffs, billy club, bullets, etc.) was draped over a closet hook. His array of cop stuff also included an item feared by all civilians: the "ticket book" he used to issue citations to anyone who did not abide by the traffic laws of the City of Tacoma. This ticket book was in his hand when he returned to the yard.

In a few minutes the offending Ford returned to the intersection and appeared to be preparing for another rapid run down our street. This time my father began walking towards the car while calling out for the driver to wait a moment. The driver, seeing a middle-aged guy approaching in his grubby yard-work attire, waited until my father was standing next to the car. I watched as the surprised driver realized that the guy in the wrinkled shirt and grass stained pants was an off-duty police officer who asked him to hand over his driver's license. The driver complied and awaited his fate. Dad had his ticket book at the ready and began writing. He returned the young driver's license nicely gift wrapped in a pink colored traffic ticket. The '40 Ford's exit down our street was much slower and quieter than the previous departures.

Dad returned to our yard with a smile and a wink directed my way.

"A ticket for reckless driving will make him think twice about returning to our neighborhood."

I don't celebrate other people's misfortune, but I do smile whenever I recall that summer afternoon working with Dad in the backyard. I wonder if the driver of the hot rod Ford is ever able to smile when his thoughts return to that day.

The Pirate Ship

When I was growing up, young boys let their fantasies run wild when they were playing. For example, we loved to emulate soldiers. We carried sticks as rifles and threw clumps of dirt as hand-grenades. We terminated many Nazi soldiers' lives at nearby Franklin Park. Next on the list was pretending to be cowboys and Indians. Short cowboys were seen all over the neighborhood and one young guy (me) had a Davy Crockett outfit complete with a real imitation leather vest and a real imitation coonskin cap. Farther down the list were cops and robbers. We chased many a bad guy down nearby alleys and, if lucky, arrested and placed them in the City Jail, a structure that strongly resembled the garage behind my house.

All of these types of characters were fine (especially Mr. Crockett), but at the top of my list and nowhere on any other neighbor kid's list was being a pirate. It was a pirate's life for me!

Hidden not very well behind the Lambert's house was a treasure trove of items that could be used to create most anything imaginable. There were piles of lumber, old pipes, sheets of plywood, large spools of wire, cases filled with glass gallon jugs and many other things that my father decided he just had to bring home. Most of the time I'd glance at his latest acquisition and perhaps come up with an idea or two of what could be done with this new truckload of castoff demolition loot.

Then something new and very useful began to accumulate: huge tables. These tables were not the kitchen or dining room types of tables. These had obviously been designed for some sort of industrial use. They were massive! The tops were made of wooden planks and the legs were columns of 4x4 or larger wood beams. They were bolted together and appeared to have previously been used to stabilize some sort of machinery. Fortunately, none of them matched. They were various sizes, heights and colors. Four or five arrived in a short time and I began to see something forming in our backyard. There before my eyes were the makings of a vessel. Not just any vessel, but a very seaworthy vessel that would have one single purpose. It would sail the high seas with *Lance the Pirate* as its captain!

My dad had lined them up next to the house perfectly. Each table was touching the next table and, just like all of the pirate ships in the movies, the tables created a deck of varying heights. The lowest level was in the middle and that was where all of the scallywags would be. I didn't know then, nor do I know now, what a scallywag was, but I knew that I certainly was not a scallywag. My guess is that scallywags caused scurvy, something else I didn't know anything about other than it was not good and that lemons, also bad, were somehow involved.

For me, being the captain of a pirate ship was a solitary occupation. In my mind I had a complete and obedient crew, but I was always alone when commanding my ship. I never invited any friends to participate in any of my pillaging and plundering on the High Seas. That way there was no questioning of my authority or any chance of a mutiny.

I did, however, occasionally take on the role of a captured British officer. My Pirate Captain was not kind to my captured British officer.

The most massive of the tables was built in a way that a long skinny board could be inserted into a slot in the side of the table. The board would then stick out and become a very respectable plank. All the pirate movies had a plank that some sorry sailor had the misfortune of "walking," and my captured British officer was going to suffer the same dunking into the shark infested backyard.

The table was stable and heavy enough that "walking the plank" did not tip the ship over. Out the doomed British officer (me) would walk, his hands tied behind his back with imaginary rope. He would stand at the end of the plank and then, with dignity and bravery, step off the end to spend eternity in Davy Jones' Locker.

Quickly I'd climb back aboard the ship and, as the Pirate Captain, smile at the successful demise of my adversary.

Woe be to any other pirates or servants of Her Majesty's Royal Navy that crossed my watery path! This pirate vessel was equipped with both muskets and cannons. The crew (again just me) was deadly with a musket (slingshot) and unfailing with a cannon (BB gun).

One battle stands out as particularly violent and victorious.

Referred to earlier were cases filled with glass gallon jugs. I removed the jugs from the boxes, lined them up along the side of the garage and filled them with water. In an instant these jugs became the side of a British frigate. I didn't have any idea what a frigate actually was other than in the movies pirates loved to sink them.

There, across the choppy sea was the enemy crew

aboard their frigate. They were scurrying about preparing to do battle with me and my crew. Fools! Had they not heard of the famous Pirate Lance, the most feared leader of scallywags in the world? Soon they would arrive at the Pearly Gates dripping wet and muttering, "If we had only known it was *Him* we were battling. We would have ported our galleys, jibbed our anchors and masted our mainsails away as fast as possible!"

"Men, prepare to give them a broadside!" I cried out. The term broadside had something to do with shooting at another ship so it seemed an appropriate thing to yell at the crew. The first musket (a slingshot loaded with a marble) was raised, aimed and fired. Direct hit! The side of the frigate sprang a massive leak and water began pouring in (out actually since it was a gallon jug full of water). Our cannons were then rolled forward and aimed. KABOOM! (Actually, the Daisy BB pistol just made a reasonably loud PFFT! Sound.) Again the British warship suffered a direct hit and was taking on even more water.

My crew continued the assault until all that was left were rings in the water where a ship had once floated, and a lot of broken glass in our soggy backyard.

The years passed and the pirate ship eventually was dismantled and taken away to reside in someone else's sea of salvaged building materials.

These days I am no longer the Captain of a pirate ship. Most of the battles that I've fought over the decades since my days as a pirate have been minor, and no slingshots, BB guns or plank walking has been necessary. But that doesn't mean that down deep in my soul there isn't a pirate wanting to command a crew of scallywags and again sail the high seas in search of treasure and illicit glory.

ARRRRRRRRR!

Rubber Remorse

It was the perfect crime! I'd surveyed the store, made a plan, assessed my chances of getting caught, committed the theft, escaped the scene of the crime and safely returned home with the "loot." So why didn't it *feel* like the perfect crime?

It all started at a Sprouse Reitz store a few blocks from my childhood home. This was a typical small "Five & Dime" store common in the 1940s, 1950s and 1960s.  It was where people bought school supplies, patterns for dresses, toys, kitchen utensils and hundreds of other items needed in their daily lives. Many items, in fact, did cost five to 10 cents.

The store was located on 6th Avenue, one of the main thoroughfares in the north portion of Tacoma. Along this street was everything that anyone needed. There were shoe stores, grocery stores, restaurants, taverns, clothing stores, gas stations, banks and all the businesses seen in every movie or TV show featuring the business area of a small town. It was my own little "Mayberry" part of Tacoma.

A popular activity for my friends and me was to walk

along several blocks of the business area and stop in some of the shops. Arlin's Shoe Store had an X-ray machine that you could stand on, slip your feet into a slot and actually X-ray your feet. Yes, there below you was the outline of your feet with the bones prominently visible.

The Victory Store had an old fashioned soda fountain (not so old then) where you could sit at the counter and enjoy a banana split or a cherry Coke. Shelly's Cycle Shop provided bicycle repair and odds & ends to accessorize your bicycle. The Central Bank offered a "Christmas Club" savings account where you could deposit your paper route or baby-sitting earnings.

All the various businesses added up to something out of a Norman Rockwell painting. I guess I kind of messed up one of his paintings.

I was roaming the three aisles of the Sprouse Reitz store with nothing in mind other than seeing what was available for five or ten cents. I was 9 or 10 years old and just tall enough to easily see what was on the counters and in the display cases. I came upon the area that displayed various office and school supplies. There were pens, pencils, tablets, erasers, paperclips, staplers and most everything else that might be needed by office workers or students. Included in the array of supplies were packages of rubber bands. I was always fascinated by rubber bands so I took a closer look.

These little rings of rubber had hundreds of uses. Besides holding things together they made great ammunition when stretched over a fingertip and released. They could be artfully laced between fingers in a way that cut off circulation and turned the fingers red and then purple. If enough rubber bands were combined they could be stretched over long distances and, best of all, could also be stretched over each other until a reasonably sized and excellently functioning rubber ball was created. Looking at the display, I felt a deep desire for the rubber bands.

I don't recall if I didn't have the nickel or dime needed to purchase the rubber bands, or if suddenly my sinful side surfaced. Either way, I made the decision to steal a package of rubber bands.

I made a plan. First came "staking out the area" and glancing around to see if I was being watched by any of the staff. It appeared that I was unnoticed. Now, how to steal the rubber bands? I chose the time-honored method of casually looking at the item. I held the package, turned it over and over, inspected it closely and then sneakily looked around to see if anyone was paying attention to me. It appeared that it was safe to perform the pilferage, so I shoved the rubber bands into my pocket and walked out the door.

In less than a few minutes I had changed from a law abiding young boy to a little thief.

I continued my wandering along 6th Avenue and eventually returned home. I went directly to my bedroom to take a closer look at the afternoon's booty.

There on my bed sat the small package of rubber bands. There was no feeling of joy as I looked at the dozens of small rubber rings. I didn't feel like I'd gotten away with something, nor was there any feeling of accomplishing anything good. I didn't need any rubber bands. Mom and Dad could provide me with a never-ending supply. The only thing I'd accomplished was to become a shoplifter. I felt terrible.

The ladies at the store had always been nice to me, and stealing from them was definitely a very bad thing to do. Anyone with any intelligence knows that a thief is eventually caught. So the decision to end my short-lived criminal career was an easy one. I carried the rubber bands out to the garbage can, discarded them and decided to once again be a law-abiding citizen. The neighborhood businesses might have merchandise stolen, but not by me.

Minor Injury - Major Pride

My years as a student at Franklin Elementary School were likely very similar to most other young boys in the 1950s. School started at 8:00 a.m. and the next seven hours consisted of increasing reading proficiency, learning basic math, developing creative talents and perhaps most importantly to many boys, playing sports.

I, on the other hand, had very little interest in any form of sports. To me, throwing, catching, hitting and kicking balls seemed a waste of energy. My passion was hanging out on the playground and laughing with other non-sports friends. There was, however, one exception to this attitude: I enjoyed playing soccer.

Franklin Elementary School was a bit unusual in that it promoted soccer, a game that was not often seen on any of Tacoma's playgrounds in the mid to late 1950s. It appealed to me because of the limited skills needed to play the game at a grade school level. Our very unsophisticated method, no doubt breaking most established rules in the world of real soccer, was to divide into two teams, pick a goalie for each side, toss the ball into the middle of the dirt field and proceed to do anything necessary that would get the ball past the opposing team's goalie and across the white chalk-line.

One of the more aggressive game activities was something we referred to as "shinning parties." A shinning party consisted of two to twenty boys bunching together as tightly as possible while kicking each other in the shins. It didn't matter who the recipient was of a well-aimed kick. Teammate or opposing team player, everyone was a target when the feet began flying. It was during a shinning party that I began my climb up one or two rungs on the school's social ladder.

The dust was flying, the preteen animal energy was building and our "party" of approximately ten boys were vigorously goose-stepping into each other. All was proceeding painfully well when I fell to the ground. I was then greeted with a kick in the face that produced a minor gusher of a nosebleed. This was during a period of my life when a change in the weather, cancellation of my favorite TV show or the price of wheat rising often resulted in my nose ejecting an impressive waterfall of blood. The nosebleeds were frequent enough that my mother took me to see our family doctor, Dr. Reynolds, to investigate. He decided that I was deficient in iron and prescribed a medicine that I can remember to this day. It was a syrup that was delicious and sweet enough to have been poured on any pile of pancakes.

But I wasn't thinking of that on the day of the shinning party when I crawled in the dust while looking into a forest of dirty and bruised ankles. The blow to my nose didn't cause much pain, but the impact was enough to open the blood-gate. My fellow shinners were concerned for my safety and, upon seeing the growing red mess, decided I needed to be escorted back to the classroom. Mrs. Gullikson, my fifth grade teacher, took one look at the damage and decided that the expertise of the school nurse was warranted.

A few things were happening to me at this time. I was receiving a lot of attention and I liked it. The amount of blood made the injury look much more serious than it actually was. I was smart enough to know that more visible blood would result in more attention and a longer reprieve from any after-recess academic requirements. Then the real payoff presented itself.

The nurse asked, "Lance, do you want us to call your parents and have them take you home?"

This was turning into one of the best days of my life! I had suffered a sports related injury that earned me just a little more respect from the mini-jocks at Franklin. I was sitting in the nurse's office rather than at my desk trying to figure out the multiplication tables. And now I was being asked if I wanted to leave school early. It was a dream come true. Little did I know that a life changing experience was soon to take place.

"Yes, I should probably go home," I responded with just the right amount of post-injury sighing in my voice.

My mother was contacted but, since she didn't drive, she was not able to come to my rescue. She called my father and, although it was a workday for him, he agreed to come pick me up and deliver me and my bleeding proboscis to my mother. The transfer was set in motion and I was sent back to the classroom to wait for my father's arrival while sitting at my desk and holding a large bandage to my nose.

Then it happened. There at the classroom door stood my father. Most anyone else's father would have arrived wearing a suit or at least slacks and a recently ironed shirt. But my father was not like everyone else's father.

Into the classroom he stepped dressed from head to toe in the coolest duds imaginable. On his feet were black shoes polished enough to reflect the lights hanging above the classroom. His perfectly pleated medium blue pants had a dark blue stripe running cuff-to-waist on each side. His shirt was dark blue with brass buttons and small, jewel-like chrome plated letters on the each collar side that read "TPD" for the Tacoma Police Department. On his head was a black eight-point hat with a shiny black brim. On his waist was a wide black belt that held handcuffs, a pouch full of bullets and (are you ready for this?) on his right hip was a

black leather holster filled with a very large gun. The cherry on top of this float was the waist-length jacket he was wearing. This was not just any jacket. This was a black leather jacket with a big silver and gold badge over his heart.

Officer Lambert

If God had walked into the room my classmates would not have been more impressed.

"I'm here to pick up my son."

My classmates looked at him in admiring amazement, looked at me and then realized that MY DAD WAS A POLICE OFFICER! I recognized the reaction and I loved it. I puffed out my chest, gathered my belongings and was escorted from the classroom by Officer Lambert.

The following day I answered questions from my classmates.

"Have you ever shot his gun?"

"Did your dad ever shoot anyone?"

"Do you get to ride in police cars?"

"What's it like having your dad be a policeman?"

I knew the answer to that last question. It was great!

Franklin Park

Going to a park is something that nearly everyone enjoys. Family outings, romantic picnics, solitary walks, whatever the reason for the visit, a park is a place of pleasure. It's also a great place for a young boy to learn about life.

Franklin Park is seven blocks from my childhood home. It adjoined Franklin Elementary School, where I first attempted to gain an education. The park consisted of several acres of wooded area next to the school, plus a well-groomed park beyond the woods. There was a baseball field, tennis courts, playground, wading pool, and open space. Just outside of the groomed areas was a small body of water, best described as a swamp, officially called Hoodlum Lake but known to the neighborhood kids as Hoodie; not Hoodie Lake, just Hoodie. The Tacoma Metro Parks website states that the now non-existent Hoodlum Lake was later called Franklin Lake; however, I've never heard anyone call it by that name.

I had many experiences at the 21-acre park, which opened in the summer of 1941—about 15 years before I began haunting it. It was a great place to meet up with friends and to make new friends. It was also a place to be cautious when someone unknown to you was approaching.

The Daily twins, Dave and Mike, were well known in the neighborhood, although it was not for their acts of kindness. Most of my friends, when seeing one or both of them at the park, would whisper, "It's the Dailys. Let's get out of here."

On one sunny Saturday afternoon my friends and I were standing around doing nothing special, which was an activity we had perfected. I was about 12 years old and most Saturdays were spent hanging out with Dale, Frankie & Johnny (the other twins in the neighborhood), Rob, James and Dan. I don't remember which friends I was with on this particular day, but I do remember there were three or four of us at the park. Someone spotted the Daily twins walking across the center of the park and warned the rest of us. I had never met the twins and only knew them by reputation. As they approached, we all wondered which one of us would be the victim of their rumored unspeakable acts of cruelty.

For some reason, surely not bravery or confidence, I began walking towards the Daily twins. As we met mid-playfield I smiled and said, "Hi, my name is Lance." Mike greeted me with indifference but Dave responded with a big smile. We began talking and then walked together. There was no indication of danger from him, and from that day on we were good friends.

Dave's leg was broken soon after this photo

Dave was, however, worthy of his reputation. He was tough and fearless. On one occasion, when we were in high school, he took care of a "problem" I was having with another student. On another occasion I had a front row seat when his fearlessness led to him breaking his leg on a ski trip. We destroyed cars together, chased girls together, and drank beer together. (It was Miller Beer, because that was the cheapest.) Best of all, we laughed together.

After high school graduation I became a college student and Dave became a soldier. I failed to complete college and he failed to complete his military term. The world lost Dave during the Vietnam War, but I was able to have one last beer with him after he was gone. It was at Mountain View Cemetery, where I visited his grave. After I left, the groundskeeper found a half-full bottle of Miller on Dave's tombstone.

Corporal David C. Daily
12/7/46 – 1/10/68

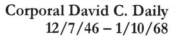

Franklin Park also provided me with the first opportunity to experience flight.

My father was always bringing home unusual and sometimes very cool items. Included on this list was the siren off of a fire engine, a flare gun (later used to accidently light the roof of a nearby gymnasium on fire), brass knuckles and, best of all, a parachute.

This surplus military freight parachute was used for

dropping supplies into remote locations so G.I.'s could have lots of yummy two-year-old biscuits or whatever edible items they needed on the battlefield. It was a bit smaller than what would be used to float a nearly full-grown soldier to the ground, making it perfect to float this 13-year-old-boy around the neighborhood.

My first foray into the wild blue yonder was at the park. I reasoned that if I spread out the open parachute on the side of the hill and began running down the hill it would inflate and do something dangerous and exciting. This was long before base jumping, parasailing, paragliding and other two digit I.Q. activities had become the passion of many thrill seeking and invincible young adults.

So there I was, repeatedly running down the hill with a parachute behind that occasionally actually filled up, rose above and transported me up and away from the ground! I floated across the park for distances of a few feet to perhaps fifty feet.

This method of travel worked well for several flights until a takeoff that resulted in the parachute canopy traveling rapidly forward instead of slowly upward. Visualize a cartoon where the hapless character's legs are spinning wildly as he attempts to keep up with whatever is forcing him to go faster than physiology allows. Put my face on that character and you have a good idea of what was going on in my life at that moment. It all came to an abrupt end when a fence surrounding the tennis courts stopped my forward momentum. I was propelled into a metal post that left a lasting impression on my chest. To this day I have a section of my ribcage that is just a bit crooked.

The parachute eventually got entangled in a tree and was ripped upon removal. There were no more flights after that, and perhaps this was a good thing.

The large hill between and above the elementary school and the park was undeveloped. This made it ideal for various childhood adventures, the number one choice being "playing army." There were a couple acres of small to medium sized trees, large shrubs and bushes, and many great hiding places and open dirt areas for close-in and direct hand-to-hand combat. Many sticks and branches were turned into rifles, machine guns and bazookas during the battles.

A road leading to the top of the hill was used by the Parks Department to truck in and dump piles of dirt. Sometimes the consistency of the dirt brought in was perfect for fighting because of the large amount of semi-solid clumps of soil, something we referred to as "dirt bombs." These we hurled through the air at the opposing forces and, upon impact, they would break apart beautifully. Those of us unfortunate enough to be on the receiving end of a toss were immediately regarded as a casualty of the battle. Getting hit in the body, or even the head, was no big deal because the dirt bombs were not very solid. A direct hit to the neck was bad because the dirt would find its way down your neck and into your clothes. Getting hit in the face was not too bad as long as your eyes were closed. If they were open, the battle was postponed until the damage was assessed. Tears were not allowed, but a trip home assisted by a friend was acceptable.

Hoodie (aka Hoodlum Lake) and the area around it was a mess. Photos from the 1940s indicate that it was well maintained back then and was utilized for fishing, boating and, best of all, swimming. Recorded history tells of a truant officer who, upon finding several boys "skinny dipping" in the lake, decided that hiding their clothes might convince them to consider wearing bathing suits in the future. The boys considered the officer's request and, upon returning for a swim the following day, were all wearing flower sacks with holes cut out for their legs.

Hoodie was not a place to swim when my crowd was strolling along the shore. Instead of a recreational body of water it had become a filthy dumping ground. There were old tires in and around the lake (swamp). Here and there were broken pieces of lawn furniture; an abandoned refrigerator resided in the bushes and broken glass was everywhere.

Boys enjoying the water on Hoodlum Lake

There was a rumor that the tires along the shoreline were once on a fire engine that had plummeted out of control into Hoodie. When I first heard the story I was young enough and gullible enough to believe it. I used to stare at the surface of the water knowing that just below the surface was a once bright red but now muddy and rusty fire engine.

None of my crowd was going to enter that body of water, but we had a lot of fun throwing anything throwable into it. Many a rock was skipped across the surface and many bottles were sent to the bottom.

The hillside that led from the hilltop battleground to the park below was fairly steep, providing two physical activities, one giggle worthy and the other Christmas card picture worthy.

During the summer months, or anytime it was dry and warm enough to go to the park, rolling down the hill was a favorite activity. My friends and I would walk up the hill, lie down sideways and begin rolling to the bottom. The distance was long enough to provide the possibility of injury, and to assure difficulty getting up and standing due to being dizzy from the hillside whirling. It was great fun!

———

Looking out a window and seeing snow on the ground was an excellent reason to grab your coat and hat, put on your gloves and run carefully to the park.

The undeveloped area of the hill had several trails that led to the developed hillside leading down into the playfield. When it snowed kids in the neighborhood would arrive dragging their sleds behind them. They would climb the developed portion of the hill, mount their sleds, and carve tracks into the hillside as they sped to the bottom. This is how the average kid went down the hill, but not how my crowd did it.

The trails in the undeveloped area doubled the distance to the bottom of the hill. It also doubled the possibility of wrack and ruin due to the shrubs and bushes on either side of the trails. The minor curves to the left and right became a little more major when speeding down the hill on a sled. Another challenge was not hitting anyone when exiting the shrubs and entering the open area of the hillside. Crashes were infrequent and injuries minor, usually just a bump, bruise or, at worst, a bloody nose when a branch or the kid in front of you stopped your forward motion.

I'm sure this winter activity on the snowy hillside resembled a scene out of a G rated Christmas movie.

I was lucky to have lived so close to a place that was constructed to make people happy. It worked.

Bare on Cedar Street

Jimmy Carlson was one of my friends in elementary school, perhaps even my best friend. Then one day, thanks to a "sleep-out," I decided to never speak to Jimmy again.

Spending the night with a friend has always been a common activity in America. Whether we called it a sleepover, an overnight, or staying over, it seems that many of us participated in this activity when we were children and young adults.

My favorite, however, was referred to as a "sleep-out." That term describes spending the night sleeping outdoors together with friends, usually in the host's back yard and usually involving two to 10 young boys. Perhaps young girls did this too, but I never heard about it if they did. That is probably because most boys are loud and silly and have the propensity to pee in the bushes and yell at imaginary wild animals that might be trying to sneak up and steal the various bags of supplies they brought along, including such essential items as candy bars, potato chips and a variety of teeth-destroying liquids.

It was one of these sleep-outs that ended my friendship with Jimmy.

Jimmy lived on South Cedar Street, three blocks away from my home on Junett Street. We set up a tent in his back yard and stocked it with the appropriate supplies. Jimmy's dad was one of the salesmen for Adams Peanut Butter, so we had a non-ending supply of peanut butter and crackers to complement the variety of goods supplied by the candy store located within two blocks.

All was going well and we did what all young boys did while sleeping out: talked, laughed, shared secrets and stuffed ourselves with delicious and unhealthy food. We were both in the sixth grade and our conversation included discussions about our classmates, what cars we would own when we were older, and anything else of interest to 11-year-olds. We also played a game called "Truth or Dare." This game consists of asking someone the question, "Truth or Dare?" to which the person being asked responds with either "Truth" or "Dare." Responding with "Truth" will result in being asked something based on a question that the asker allegedly knows the answer to. If the correct answer is not given, the person being asked then has to perform some act dictated by the person asking the "Truth" question. Responding with the answer, "Dare" means that the person being asked is willing to do an action that they are dared to do.

We finally fell asleep on Friday evening and early the next morning Jimmy and I woke up in the tent and began playing a vigorous game of "Truth or Dare." It was Jimmy's turn to ask and, when given the choice, I responded with "Truth." This response was the beginning of the end of our friendship. I remember his "Truth" question as if he'd asked it yesterday.

"How many bricks are there in the Empire State Building?" he asked. I had no idea and it was very likely he didn't know the answer either. I do not remember my answer, but Jimmy was able to convince me that he knew the right answer and that the answer I had given was wrong. Now I *had* to do whatever he told me to do because, after all, I was in the 6th grade and there was no "chickening out" allowed for any self-respecting 6th grader.

"OK Jimmy, what do I have to do?" I asked. My young life was about to change.

"You have to take off all of your clothes, run out to the front of my house, touch my parent's car and run back!" This seemed a bit drastic to me, but rules are rules and there was no refusing this unavoidable requirement of the game.

It was about 6:00 a.m. and all was very quiet in the neighborhood. I felt confident nobody was around and the likelihood of being seen running around naked was nearly zero. I was wrong.

I accepted the bare-cheeked challenge and quickly dropped my clothing into a pile. I parted the tent flaps, scoped out the route to and from the car and commenced the sprint. It was a short distance to the car, probably no more than 40 feet. My bare feet skimmed across the back yard, slapped down on the sidewalk and guided me successfully to the back of Mr. & Mrs. Carlson's car. The mission was accomplished and now all I had to do was

scamper quickly back to the cover provided by the tent where I would be the recipient of new respect from Jimmy.

Jimmy Carlson's house

As I turned away from the car I looked up at the house and there, looking out of the dining room window, was Jimmy's mother. She was staring down at me with a look of shock and horror on her face. It was obvious that she did not approve of a naked, skinny kid running across her yard.

I sprinted back to the tent and got dressed while telling Jimmy that his mother had just seen me touching her car while naked. I do not recall what we thought might happen, but I do remember very well what did happen later that day.

Our sleep-out ended and I packed my sleeping bag, grabbed some leftover supplies and trekked the three blocks back to my house. My mother greeted me and asked, "Did you have fun spending the night in Jimmy's back yard?"

"I think so," I responded.

That afternoon the phone rang. My mother called out, "Lance, the phone is for you. It's Jimmy." I didn't expect the conversation to be anything other than 6th grade boy small talk. What I heard Jimmy say still echoes in my ears 60 years later.

"My mother says I can't play with you anymore."

I could not believe what I was hearing! Jimmy and I were the best of friends. I was at his house several times a week. His mother made me snacks. His dad tousled my hair. Jimmy shared his toys with me and we began learning how to build model cars together. We were pals.

I asked what this was all about and he responded, "I'm not supposed to talk to you or be your friend anymore. It's because my mom saw you running naked in front of our house."

I began to get mad for several reasons. Did his mother think I was some kind of weird kid because she saw me running around naked in public? Looking back, that does seem to be a possible reason for her concern; however, to me at the time it all seemed pretty innocent and it was not a reason to forbid Jimmy to play with a kid that was her son's good friend.

"Did you tell her that you still wanted to be my

friend?" I asked hopefully.

"No, because she won't let me be your friend no matter what I say," he responded.

Now I was angry with him for not standing up for me since, after all, he was the instigator of the naked dash to his parent's car. Yes, I was a willing participant in the alleged indecent incident, but I was only living up to the rules of the game. There was not much discussion after that and we ended the conversation.

I gave it some thought and decided that the event was both very unfair and very embarrassing for me. I was not some naughty kid, just a kid playing a game that perhaps went a bit too far. I therefore decided to accept his decision to accept his mother's decision. I also decided to no longer be Jimmy's friend.

From that day forward Jimmy and I didn't speak to each other, at least not until a couple of years ago when we connected on Facebook. Now, we occasionally exchange a comment about our days back in Tacoma. It's been nice communicating with him and looking back on it makes me realize that we should not have let the event cause the end of our friendship.

So I have a dare for you, Jimmy: Call me. I have a great tent and lots of peanut butter! And, according to Google, there are over 10 million bricks in the Empire State Building.

New Knots

I was 12 years old when my siblings and I became children from a "broken home."

It was obvious at the time that Mom and Dad had been having problems in their marriage for several years. There were no screaming battles that I was aware of, just hushed discussions behind their closed bedroom door that usually resulted in Dad leaving the house and Mom emerging from the bedroom with eyes still moist from tears. I never questioned the reason for this and perhaps those years were when I developed my survival skill of avoiding confrontations. I did my best to live the life of a young boy doing young boy activities. One day this all came to an end.

My sister Judy asked me to go for a walk with her, and that was when I found out that our house's population was going to decrease by one.

"Mom and Dad are getting a divorce" she said cautiously. It didn't come as much of a surprise and I accepted it with very little sadness. It seemed like a simple solution to my parents' problem.

I don't think I responded with much more than, "Oh, OK."

Sometime prior to all of this Dad had met Jean Taylor and fallen in love with her. She was a mother of two, a nursing school student and working at the Narrows Drive-In restaurant to pay bills. One day I was at the drive-in with my father and he introduced me to Jean. She seemed nice and I did notice that my order of fries was extra generous. A year or two later she officially became my stepmother.

Along with acquiring another mother I acquired a stepbrother, John Taylor, and a stepsister, Dixie Taylor. But I lived with my birthmother, never with Dad's other family.

John and I were classmates at school, although we barely knew each other and ran around in different crowds. He was a nice guy but we never developed a brotherly relationship.

Additional fries and then an additional mother

Dixie was older and out of school. She was pretty and a bit of a rebel. I liked that about her, though we were together only a few times.

Mom spent a few years crying over the divorce, and then recovered enough to fall in love with her beautician. They married and, I assume, she no longer had to pay for having her hair done.

Acquiring a stepdad included acquiring another

stepbrother and two more stepsisters. Russell Bass, known to his friends as Rusty, was a year younger than me and a year behind me in school. I knew him prior to our parents uniting because he and his family lived only one block away from us. I'd had little interaction with him previously other than once taking a baseball bat away from him (I gave it back). It took a short adjustment period to establish our relationship after his dad and my mom tied the nuptial knot. There was one minor scuffle, after which we got along well.

My additional two new stepsisters, Miffin and Robin Bass, moved to California to live with their mother after their parents' divorce. We never lived together, but I liked both of them. I'm probably one of very few people who have a family member named Miffin that is not a cat.

A lot of heartache was involved in these two divorces, but some good came of them. My mother and stepfather were a much happier couple than Mom's previous arrangement, and the same can be said for my dad's new marriage. There were no hard feelings on my part and life went on in the two new households.

My father wanted me to live with him, but I refused the offer for two reasons. One, his house was a dump. He wasn't poor but it sure looked like it. I also didn't feel like I would have been a good fit with his new family. It's a choice I have never regretted.

The choice I did make seemed like a reasonably good decision. Rusty and I coexisted peaceably and we had some laughs together. Bob, my stepdad, was easy to get along with and, most importantly, he made my mother happy.

By the time all of this happened my sister Judy had gotten married and my brother Lynn was serving as a Latter Day Saints (Mormon) missionary in Australia, followed by being a student at Brigham Young University's campus on the island of Oahu in Hawaii. Back then it was known as The

Church College of Hawaii, an academic institution where a few years later the student directory included my name. Lynn transferred to the Provo, Utah campus after two years in Hawaii.

Divorce is considered a bad thing in society and is seen as a failure and, for many, an embarrassing chapter (book?) in a person's life history. For others it is the opportunity to leave behind years of sadness and begin a future that will, hopefully, be filled with happiness.

Mom and Dad both smiled a lot more after they each tied their new knots.

Fill'er Up?

There are several things I miss about the 1950s. Near the top of the list is the neighborhood gas station.

On the northeast corner of South 12th and Pine in Tacoma was a Signal service station that opened for business on December 15th, 1950. *Paul's Signal Service* had all the cool stuff you'd expect -- new and used tires everywhere, rusty signs pitching tire repair and bulk oil, a hissing and clanking pop machine and, best of all, Paul's best employee: George. He was right out of Mayberry -- dirty coveralls, pointed attendant's hat, grease under his fingernails and a great attitude. He believed that if you kept Mrs. Conklin's Buick running properly she'd keep coming back for gas and repairs. Both Paul and George felt that marking up items more than ten percent was criminal. And, much to my delight, he was willing to let a very young car nut kid hang out at the station.

I'd ride my Schwinn Black Phantom bicycle there once or twice a week just to watch him work. There wasn't a lot of conversation coming from George. Sitting quietly with him in the "office" shed waiting for customers to arrive was all I needed.

He finally put me to work sweeping the garage and parking lot. I was thrilled to be "working" at a real gas station and quickly worked my way up to official tire stacker, floor grease scraper and window cleaner. I was even allowed to visit the most mysterious place at any 1950s station -- the "grease pit." This was the pit in the concrete floor where you went to change a car's oil or work on the undercarriage. It was wet from spilled and leaking oil, a little dangerous and a place where only grownups were allowed.

I cared very little that George never paid me any money because being able to hang out at the station was payment enough.

In my eyes, the prestige job was actually pumping gas into customer's cars. As far as I was concerned this was as good as being paid money. George and I would be sitting in the office when a car would drive up to the pump. I'd look at him apprehensively and wait for his quiet nod. When he nodded towards the car I'd race out and ask, "Fill'er up?"

Suddenly I was the most important 12-year-old kid in the neighborhood. Not only could I closely watch the gas pump gauge and stop at exactly $2.00, but I could remove the nozzle without spilling a drop. This was the most exciting car-related activity that I'd ever been a part of.

That summer was one of the best in my memory. As I grew older, I realized the need to get a real job if I was ever going to own a real car. I became a pin setter at the Elks Club bowling alley, got a paper route and did odd jobs around the neighborhood. Before long I had saved up $125 and bought a 1948 Chev Fleetline Aero Sedan.

I bet you can guess where I bought my first tank of gas.

Slot-Car Surprise

Christmas was drawing near and there was only one thing on my list; a slot-car racing set.

I first noticed slot-car sets in the late 1950s, and by 1960 the desire to own one had surpassed the desire for anything else I'd ever wanted. These sets included several long flat pieces of black plastic with a metal edged slot running down the center end-to-end, along with two small plastic cars equipped with electric motors. Most sets also included tiny fences and signs to help create a more realistic looking miniature racetrack. Additionally, two hand-held mechanisms were included that controlled the speed of the tiny racecars.

The slot car hobby took America by storm and I wanted to be in the middle of it all. For a car crazy kid this was an exciting way to let your imagination put you in the driver's seat on race day.

The cost of slot-car sets put them at the upper end of my family's Christmas gift budget. I couldn't afford to buy a set and my mother (recently divorced and unemployed) was not likely able to either. That did not stop me from letting her know at every opportunity that all I wanted for Christmas was a slot-car racing set. As the days dropped off the calendar and the holidays grew closer I stepped up my relentless hinting.

"Mom, look! There's an ad in this magazine for the new Aurora 'Model Motoring' slot-car set."

"Mom, it says in the newspaper that Rhodes Department Store is going to have a sale on slot-car sets!"

"Dan and James have slot-car sets. If I had one we could race on each other's tracks. Mom, did you hear me? Mom?"

Then something began happening as Santa's arrival grew nearer. I began getting hints from my mother.

"Lance, I think you are really going to like your Christmas present!"

Was this going to be under the Christmas tree?

"You won't be getting a lot this year because you are getting one very special present."

A few days before Christmas the biggest and most promising hint of all came from my sister. "You are getting something that you will be very excited about. And it is something that Mom *has to put together.*"

Put together!? What else could it be other than a slot-car set? The track had to be *put together.* I was so very excited.

I imagined coming downstairs on Christmas morning and seeing a large slot-car set laid out on the living room floor. There would be at least two big curves and two straight-aways. No doubt the miniature cars would be bright festive colors and would travel at scale speeds in excess of 200 miles-per-hour. I would spend all of Christmas day squeezing the hand held throttle and being victorious time after time as my brother, sister and mother attempted to compete against me.

One of the first things I'd do would be to call Dan and James to let them know of receiving the gift of my dreams. We'd make plans to get together in the next few days to race on each other's tracks.

This was going to be the best Christmas ever!

Now all I had to do was wait for the big day. I went to bed on Christmas Eve and fell asleep with visions of little sugar plum colored, electric powered plastic cars racing around my new slot car-track.

Early the next morning my eyes popped open and I smiled upon realizing that my wish was about to come true. I jumped out of bed, ran down the stairs and joined the rest of the family in the kitchen.

There stood Mom, my brother Lynn and my sister Judy.

"Are you kids ready to see what is under the tree?" my mother asked.

We all smiled and my sister winked at me knowing how happy I'd be when I saw what was waiting for me on the living room floor.

We all walked out of the kitchen and into the living room together.

Something didn't appear right. The floor was not covered with strips of winding black plastic. Instead there was something tall and box-shaped hidden under a sheet.

Yes, I suppose it could be a slot-car racing set still in the box, but the shape under the sheet was wrong.

My mother and sister walked to either side of the box, took hold of the sheet and pulled it back. Unfortunately what was revealed was not a slot-car racing set.

During the previous year I had saved up enough money to buy a record player. It was a style that was common at that time; it looked like a typewriter case with a turntable inside. When the top of the case was opened the turntable and controls were accessible. The record player had been sitting on my floor, and this had worked just fine. I'd sit on the floor, go through my limited record collection and play the recordings of my choice.

Apparently my mother did not think the floor was the proper place for my record player to reside.

There before me, in front of the Christmas tree, presented proudly on each side by my mother and sister, was a bright, shiny brass-plated metal and wire record player stand. It had a shelf on top to place the record player and a shelf underneath to stack records. It was a very nice record player stand; however, it was not a slot-car racing set.

How did I deal with this letdown? This was not what I'd spent months grooming my mother to purchase for me. There she stood looking so very proud. Mom was not mechanically talented and it had likely been a challenge for her to put this brass-plated beauty together. My sister had a look on her face that indicated she expected me to be overwhelmed with happiness and gratitude.

I loved my mother and I loved my sister. It was easy to see that this moment was very meaningful to both of them. This *not a slot-car* Christmas present was likely not within my mother's gift budget. She had done something extra special for me.

Perhaps having a slot-car racing set was not really so

important. Mom needed a little extra happiness at this time in her life and this was an opportunity for me to give it to her.

"That is the most beautiful record player stand that I've ever seen! I can't wait to get it into my room, put the record player on it and stack the records in it. Thanks Mom!"

My mother was very happy that Christmas. Many years later I bought a slot-car set.

Eddy Hanson's Sister

I'm so old that I used to hang out at a real drugstore with a real soda fountain. Yes, the kind that starlets are rumored to be discovered at, the kind at which dozens of '50's era teenagers lined up on stools while sharing a milkshake with two straws and looking all goo-goo-eyed at their "steady."

My particular soda fountain was on South 12th Street, a place that in my preteen years was always exciting to visit. In a one-block area between South Junett Street and South Pine Street there was a bakery, five & dime store (kind of an early version of a dollar store) and Fowler's drug store. My friend Dan's dad owned the bakery, and I'd occasionally help Dan clean the place up. My pay was all of the day-old bakery goods that I could stuff into my pre-pubescent face. The five & dime next door had aisles overflowing with office supplies, sewing merchandise, toys, candy and, depending on the season, a huge supply of cheap decorations. One store filled my stomach, one filled my pockets and the third filled my imagination.

I've been crazy about cars since birth. If it had wheels I was interested in it. But when I was nearing my teens a new interest arose. The new interest, though not as desirable as a cool car, was a human of the opposite gender. Yes, I had discovered that girls were fun to be with.

Most of the girls I was around were classmates and/or neighbor kids my own age. I liked Mary Kay O'Reily (the first girl I ever kissed), Janet Butcher (the recipient of my first heroic act when I got her foot unstuck from a tree limb) and Patty Julian, the prettiest girl in the neighborhood with the most overprotective dad. They were all very nice, but they were not Eddy Hanson's sister.

Eddy's sister was four years older, and when you are a 12-year-old boy, a 16-year-old-girl is *much* older. She was very pretty, in high school and much wiser due to being alive 33.3% longer than I had been. She'd also acquired some attributes that I was beginning to notice on girls.

Saturdays were a pretty good day when I was this age. There was time to ride my Schwinn, hang out with friends and, frequently, make the four-block trip to tour the pleasure dens of 12th Street. I'd walk to the bakery and get some free pastries, cruise the five & dime (the signs always used the "&") to see what item I needed to save my money for, and then walk 50 feet to the real destination; Fowler's Drug Store.

The first pleasure was the huge apothecary bottles displayed in the window. They were full of colored water and appeared to me as beautiful as any cathedral's stained glass windows. I'd admire the kaleidoscope display as I approached the door. Upon entering I'd be impressed by the hospital-like cleanliness of the drug store displays and the rows of well placed items. However, none of these items were my target.

Each visit to Fowler's had two purposes: literary and carnal. The literary purpose was fulfilled with a long period of thumbing through the various car magazines. The grownup magazines were mildly entertaining. *Road & Track*, *Motor Trend* and a few others provided information about a few cars that I cared about. The real knowledge I sought was provided by the "Little Books," such as *Car Craft*, *Rod & Custom* and *Custom Rodder*. I'd get my fill of the latest custom car creations and then get to satisfy my craving for the second most interesting thing in my life; Eddy's sister.

I was usually broke during these early years, but that didn't stop me from seeking items that usually required a few coins to obtain. My technique was simple: say hi to Eddy's sister, who worked at the drugstore soda fountain. She'd smile and nod to a stool. I'd settle in, shyly make some comments about goings-on in the neighborhood and casually mention that I didn't have any money. She reacted by providing me with free refreshment.

Car magazines, cherry Cokes and Eddy's sister

Cherry Cokes were all the rage in my town, along with a lime-flavored drink called a Greenriver. The appeal of a Greenriver was lost on me, but a cherry Coke was fine wine to this youngster. She'd mix me a drink and, if it was slow at the soda bar, give me all of her attention. At this point I was overflowing with custom car knowledge, cherry flavored Coke-a-Cola and, best of all, a newly discovered interest in a pretty girl 33.3% older than I was.

I do not recall how many times I was able to indulge in this exquisite combination, but it must have been a few because I recall the enjoyment of the cola based drink and the minor revulsion caused by the green concoction, all preceded by wrinkling several pages of various automotive publications. Of course gazing at the teenager serving drinks from behind the counter was the main purpose of my sojourn to South 12th Street.

The infatuation with Eddy's sister eventually passed. It has been so long ago that, as is obvious, I can't even remember her name. She remained four years older than I was and, as older people often do, she created a life somewhere else that did not include providing me with free cherry Cokes.

All is not lost, however. There are cherry Cokes in my refrigerator, old "little books" in my garage, and a tiny place in my heart where Eddy Hanson's sister lives.

A Matchless Fire

My brother Lynn has been and continues to be an automotive mentor in my life. He's had several cool cars and motorcycles during his lifetime, and he's an expert at transforming a pile of parts and pieces into a running vehicle. The process has usually gone well, or at least until the occasional unexpected thing happens. I guess starting a fire in the house would be one of the unexpected things.

Lynn acquired a motorcycle when he was 16 years old. What he actually acquired was a bike in rough shape along with a bunch of parts that had previously been a 1952 Matchless 500 Twin. He was, like most of his peers, a near penniless teenager with a part-time job and the need for some type of transportation. His only option was to do his best to turn this pile of parts into a complete and running motorcycle.

At that time Stately Lambert Manor had a collapsing garage with a leaking roof and no garage door. Bringing the Matchless back to life in that structure was not going to happen, so Lynn used the only other option available -- the basement.

Our home's basement was below ground. A flight of concrete steps descending from the alley was utilized to gain entry from outside of the house. Getting Lynn's motorcycle and the various parts into the basement took a bit of strength and a few trips, but everything necessary found its way into the subterranean space needed to resurrect the Matchless.

This project was interesting enough to me that I would occasionally park my 12-year-old self nearby and watch as he did the mysterious things that were necessary to breathe life back into the motorcycle. When I became bored I'd walk up the wooden stairs leading to the kitchen and go about my important pre-teen business. Little did I know that the wooden stairs within the house and the concrete stairs leading to the outside of the house from the basement would soon be the cause of ruin and rescue.

One weekend afternoon my big brother was putting the finishing touches on the Matchless while my mother and I were engaged in some activity in the kitchen. We were not aware that Lynn's project was nearing completion and would be ready that day to emerge from the basement womb and out into the world. He did face one dilemma; this re-birth would only happen when he figured out how to transfer the motorcycle from its subterranean location to the outside world via the concrete steps leading up from the basement. The solution seemed obvious to him; start the Matchless and ride it up the concrete basement stairs.

The firefighter's destination

Our mother and I were still working in the kitchen when we heard something that sounded like a gunshot. The noise was the result of my brother trying to start the motor. His attempt resulted in a flurry of activity in the Lambert residence.

Upon hearing the blast I walked to the basement door and looked down the stairs. This was the same moment my brother came running up the stairs. "The motorcycle is on fire!" he shouted as he raced past me. I glanced down the staircase and, sure enough, there were flames engulfing the rear of the motorcycle. Apparently my brother had somehow set a match to the Matchless. My mother, being older and, therefore, a bit smarter than her sons, did the appropriate thing by calling the fire department.

The fire had begun when Lynn tried to start the engine. He stood on the kick-starter, pushed hard with his foot and was then startled when the Matchless responded with a loud backfire. This same backfire set fire to some gas soaked rags that he'd been using to clean off some of the engine's grime. It must have been a Rube Goldberg type of progression; foot goes on kick-starter, kick-starter goes down, back-fire flame exits the exhaust pipes, pile of rags catch on fire, brother jumps off of motorcycle, flames quickly grow, motorcycle mechanic runs up the stairs, little brother opens door, big brother runs past, little brother's mouth opens wide and eyes get very large…

Lynn raced into the kitchen, filled a pot with water and ran back down to the flames. Our home was located only three blocks from the fire station so the firemen arrived quickly. By then Lynn had put out the flames and was sitting on the wooden steps assessing the damage. It is common knowledge that water usually will not put out a gasoline fire. Fortunately, those gas-soaked rags didn't seem to know that.

I excitedly watched the arrival of the firefighters as they came running down the outside basement stairs. What impressed me most was how quickly our home went from being a Norman Rockwell type of scene to a painting resembling Dante's Inferno.

The good news is that the smoking Matchless was carried out of the basement by the firemen. The damage was mostly superficial and it was easily repaired.

What did the Lamberts gain from this experience? Lynn continued repairing motorcycles but didn't again try to ride any of them up a set of stairs. I learned that repairs should be done in a garage, rather than in a basement, and that living three blocks from a fire station was a good thing. My mother learned that her sons' romance with gas-powered vehicles could be fiery in more ways than one.

Wedgees in the Window

I needed new shoes and it was up to me to buy them. There was a problem, however; I was broke.

I was 13 years old and my mother had said, "I have no money to buy clothes for you so you'll have to find the money to buy anything you need." She was not being cruel or unreasonable; she had no money. She didn't have a job and the support money from my father was rarely paid. What money that did arrive had to be used for food and other necessities. New clothes for the Lambert siblings were not considered necessities. I totally understood my mother's dilemma and accepted the responsibility of clothing myself.

The school year was about to start and everyone knows that a new school year starts with new school clothes. My limited wardrobe was sufficient and it was no big deal to me, with the exception that I needed new shoes. Not wanted, needed. I was placing cardboard inserts in my shoes to stop the passage of dirt from the ground, through the holes in the soles and into the shoes.

Rosalie's Department Store, located a few blocks from home, had a pair of "wedgees" displayed in the window. Wedgees were, and I suppose still are, a shoe that has a continuous flat sole. There is no difference between the heel and sole, just one big slab. Wedgees had been very popular a year or two before this pair found its way to the Rosalie's window display. As far as wedgees go this pair was not attractive. Besides being out of style they were white leather with a zipper up the side of each shoe. The word "nerd" did not exist at the time, but these shoes were definitely nerdy. They did have one attractive feature; they were on sale for $3.

People are always talking about how cheap things were when they were younger. In 1960, the year of this shoe saga, gas was 25 cents a gallon, burgers were 20 cents and a decent pair of men's leather shoes were about $10. At $3 the wedgees in the window were a bargain.

Here's the dilemma: I had very little money for shoes but had just enough to buy these shoes. They were, however, so out of style that I would surely face ridicule from my peers if I arrived at school wearing these white zip-up wedgees. It was time to get creative.

I bought the shoes and walked a few doors down the street to Arlin's Shoes. They sold shoe dye that would magically turn the shoes into a nerdy pair of black wedgees instead of a nerdier pair of white wedgees. I bought the dye and transformed them into shoes that were new, functional and might go unnoticed by my classmates. The dye process was a success but the camouflage job was a failure. They were still zip-up wedgees.

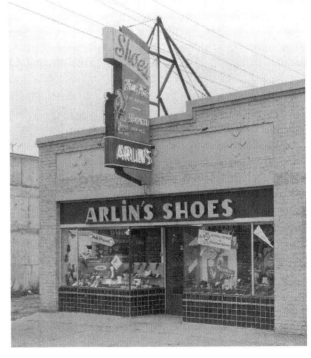

The new school year at Jason Lee Junior High School started and friends and acquaintances arrived in their new fall wardrobes. My lack of a crisp new shirt and blue jeans went unnoticed, but my wedgees, unfortunately, did not. I received a bit of good-natured ribbing from my buddies and a little not-so-good-natured ribbing from other classmates. Fortunately, in a short time the out-of-style shoes became just a pair of shoes that were no longer worthy of any comments.

The odd thing is that I loved these wedgees. They were excellent quality and very comfortable. But more than that, I felt very proud that I had found a way to no longer have to put cardboard in my shoes.

SnoBalls and Sisters

What smells good and is pretty? Wonder Bread and the Vadnais sisters.

The house I lived in from age 2 to age 15 was located nine blocks from the Continental Baking Company, makers of Wonder Bread. This large facility provided five wonderful things to the neighborhood.

First, the building itself, though being a large commercial structure situated on the edge of a mostly residential neighborhood, was beautiful and, in my opinion, added a little bit of class to the area.

Continental Baking at S. 7th & Sprague, home of Wonder Bread

Second on the list was the smell; it smelled just like a bakery. Duh! The best smells in the world are a baby in a clean diaper, fresh cut grass and a bakery. Imagine a baby holding a plate of just-out-of-the-oven chocolate chip cookies while sitting on a freshly cut lawn. Imagine the fragrance when the bakery's landscapers arrived for the weekly grass trimming.

Third, and this is a good one, was the thrift store within the bakery. The shelves were stocked with loaves of Wonder Bread (Builds Strong Bodies 12 Ways!), Twinkies, Hostess Cupcakes and, best of all, SnoBalls. These delicacies were so cheap that they were almost being given away for free.

Number four is part of number three but is so fantastic that it deserves its own separate number. SnoBalls, as some readers may recall, were chocolate cupcakes with a cream filling that had one more part that made them the best food creation in the history of the world. They had some sort of sweet spongy covering that was sprinkled with bits of coconut. No doubt the creator of this tasty combination now resides in Heaven's best neighborhood.

Each package included a white colored SnoBall and a pink colored SnoBall. There was only one proper way to consume a package of Sno Balls, at least according to my personal research and experience. First I opened the package and removed the white SnoBall. This I ate first because the pink one was the best and, therefore, was saved for last. I guess it was the pink dessert to be enjoyed after the white SnoBall meal. Furthermore, I NEVER just took a bite out of the entire SnoBall. NEVER! There was a correct procedure to follow.

The cake and coconut concoction was manufactured in a manner that allowed the outer spongy and coconut-sprinkled portion to be easily peeled away. When removed, it stayed together and looked like a little white or pink igloo. The first SnoBall skin (white) I carefully ate and enjoyed while savoring the anticipation of biting into the now naked and waiting chocolate and cream cupcake, to be followed by repeating the same procedure with the pink SnoBall.

SnoBalls came two to a package and that is how God and Continental Baking wanted them to be eaten. The cupcakes were also not meant to be shared! I'm sure somewhere on the package's small print it stated, "Not to be shared under any circumstances! Anyone sharing this product will be fined and/or imprisoned for a period of not less than the rest of their life!"

OK, I've saved the best thing the Wonder Bread Bakery shared in the neighborhood for last. The bakery was located one block from the Vadnais sisters' house. Elaine and Evonne Vadnais, like a package of SnoBalls, were beautiful. And, like the pink and white SnoBalls, they were similar in appearance but different enough to each have their own separate appeal.

On Mondays after school or in the summer my mother would say, "Lance, here's a dollar. Go to the bakery and get ten loaves of bread. And here's a nickel to buy something for you." Mondays were always 10 loaves for a dollar day at the bakery.

The pink and white pleasure balls and other pastries cost more than a nickel at the grocery store, but the stale ones or overstock at the bakery were sold at closeout prices in the thrift store. Mom didn't have to ask twice when I was given this chore.

I left the house and began the walk easterly along South 8th Street. About two blocks from the bakery the Vadnais house would come into view. At the same time the intoxicating smell of the various items cooking in the giant ovens began taking control of my senses. I was overwhelmed by the anticipation of possibly getting a peek at one or both of the Vadnais sisters and soon thereafter consuming the SnoBalls. I was young when my mother sent me to the bakery, but not too young to appreciate the beauty of girls.

If the Vadnais family porch was empty then I'd be just a little let down, continue to the bakery and hope that my return trip home might provide the opportunity to see the sisters.

After arriving at the bakery I'd spend very little time in the thrift store because there were no decisions to be made. I'd grab a cart, toss in 10 loaves of bread, reach for the least beat-up package of SnoBalls and walk to the counter. There were other pastries to choose from, including Twinkies and Hostess Cupcakes. Most of my friends were addicted to Hostess Cupcakes, but I knew that was because they were not as sophisticated as I was when it came to appreciating the finer combinations of sugar and fat. I'd make my purchase and head for home filled with anticipation for the soon-to-be-enjoyed flavorful delights of the SnoBalls and the visual delights of the nearby pretty siblings.

Carrying 10 loaves of bread was a bit awkward, but the reward made the effort worthwhile. Five loaves fit perfectly in one shopping bag and five in another, with one bag being topped by a package of SnoBalls. The upside of carrying two bags filled with bread was that it provided camouflage while I scanned the area for the Vadnais sisters. I didn't want to be too obvious and, as a result, likely embarrass myself.

On most trips the Vadnais veranda was empty, but on a few trips I struck either silver or gold. Silver was when either Elaine or Evonne was on the porch. Gold was when they both were outside and observable to passersby.

If one or both of the Vadnais sisters were on the porch and spotted me I'd look their way, swallow and awkwardly say, "Um, hi." That was not much of a winning conversation, but at least it was some sort of communication. Sometimes I managed to greet them with a complete sentence. "Um, hi. I, um, went to the bakery." Considering how young I was this was some pretty smooth talking if you ask me.

The reward of getting SnoBalls meant that there was never a bad trip to the bakery. Even when I didn't spot the Vadnais sisters, the journey included the cherished ritual of stripping the spongy outer layer away from the cupcake, making it disappear and then devouring the remaining ingredients.

Epworth Methodist Church

The route to the bakery included passing the Epworth Methodist Church located on the corner of South 8th and

Anderson Street. On my return from the bakery, regardless of success or lack thereof in Vadnais sister spotting, I'd walk around the north side of the church to a less frequented entry to the building. There I'd lay my burden down, remove the package of SnoBalls and proceed to open the parcel of pleasure. I consumed the contents in the manner previously described while taking in my surroundings. Within view was Patty Julian's house across the street from the church. Patty, a young lady closely watched over by her parents, was every bit as pretty as Elaine and Evonne. She was also right there on my path to and from the Wonder Bread Bakery. Perhaps, I thought, it was time to expand my bakery experience and try the new Hostess Fruit Pies that the Wonder Bread thrift bakery was selling. And how often, I wondered, did Patty Julian sit on her porch?

Marquee Delight

Like most of my peers, I started looking for ways to make some money at an early age. Before the age of 16 (legal working age in Washington State) I had many "jobs" that paid little, or even nothing, but some provided a privilege or perk. I searched gutters, ditches and alleys for beer bottles and pop bottles to return for the deposit, helped clean up at a local gas station, was a pin setter in a bowling alley, helped maintain a neighbor's yard, cleaned up at a local bakery, sold donuts and soap door to door, had a paper route, and did many other activities that brought a little cash into my hands.

One of my favorite jobs with the best perks was changing the marquee every week at the Sunset Theater, located a few blocks from my home. I'd walk out on scaffolding and hang up the metal letters that told the world what movie would begin playing the next day. I did not get paid in cash for this work. Instead I received unlimited entry into the theater and unlimited bags of popcorn. It was a great deal! The Sunset Theater was one of the most popular hangouts in my neighborhood, and the back row helped me learn some pleasant things about girls. Neither the girls nor the popcorn were the best part of the job; it was the view from the marquee's catwalk.

We've all seen film footage of brightly lit movie theater marquees. It's often in black and white and shot from above the marquee. The camera is pointed down at the sign and in the background are many automobiles passing below. This view always seems to be exciting, especially if you enjoy old cars and going to the movies.

Former Sunset Theater in 2016

Changing the marquee started with being handed a piece of paper with the upcoming movie's title. I was 13 years old at the time and not a good speller, so I needed a note from the manager to ensure the public knew that the movies playing inside (always a double-bill) were "Psycho" and not "Sico," or "Exodus" and not "Xadus." I'd then go into the storage area, put the appropriate letters in a box and head towards the window that led out to the catwalk on both sides of the marquee. The change was made on Thursday evenings to publicize the new double bill that started every Friday. It was exciting and always felt just a little dangerous being on the catwalk, though only a few feet below was the roof over the ticket seller's booth. The real thrill, though, was seeing the cars pass on the street below the brightly lit marquee.

This was 1960 and I loved every car on every street. I would stand at the end of the catwalk and admire the marquee's light reflecting on the cars that were passing below on 6th Avenue. Every car's chrome trim shone like diamonds and every car's taillights looked like glowing rubies. At that time cars from the 1940s and early 1950s were still being driven and my imagination placed me behind the steering wheel of many of them. The marquee could be changed quickly but I did the job slowly so I could admire the cars passing below.

The fun on the catwalk would end and then the fun in the theater would begin. It felt so special to be able to come and go as I pleased without having to pay thirty-five-cents for a ticket to see the movies. Not only did I get unlimited amounts of popcorn, but I also was allowed to go behind the counter to get it myself. On a few occasions I'd return to the roof with a bag of popcorn. There I'd sit watching the cars passing below while contemplating what car that I'd one day be driving past the Sunset Theater. It was a 1948 Chevrolet.

Jail Doors

Most people will do anything to stay out of a jail cell. My brother and I, on the other hand, snuck into a police station and intentionally locked ourselves in a cell.

It happened in 1960, two years after Tacoma's new County City Building was dedicated and opened to the public. It was the location of the majority of the city's governmental departments, including the Police Department and the new jail. The building that previously housed the police station and jail cells had been closed and boarded up for a few years, waiting for remodeling into a multi-purpose office building. What a few years prior had been a busy municipal facility was now just an old spooky-looking vacant building. It was also a building that beckoned to two brothers looking for adventure.

I was 13 years old at the time and my brother Lynn was 17. We were old enough to know that sneaking into the old police station was both foolish and illegal. We were, however, young enough to think that it seemed like a great adventure. It didn't bother either of us that our father, a career police officer with Tacoma's Finest, might not approve of his sons' jailhouse caper.

We climbed aboard the family's trusty Lambretta 150 motor scooter and headed towards downtown Tacoma. Upon arrival we parked the scooter as inconspicuously as possible and began looking for a way to get into the old jail. Much to our surprise we found the huge castle-like front doors unlocked.

The old building, a large structure that appeared to have been designed by a committee rather than an architect, had been the location of the Police Department, the county jail, and various other governmental agencies. It was known as, appropriately, the "Public Safety Building." We called it the "Lambert Brothers Funhouse." It was late Saturday afternoon when we entered the now unsafe Public Safety Building. There was remodeling rubble everywhere and eerie lights and shadows cast on the walls from the uncovered windows. It was great! We crept down the halls, peeked around corners and wondered where our father had spent most of his time here when he was not out on the streets arresting bad guys. We worked our way to the jail portion of the building and there made a discovery -- the jail's cell doors were still operational. There was electrical power in the building and the system of opening and closing the cell doors

was still functional. We located a huge metal handle and it was just like what is seen in the movies -- push the handle one direction and several cell doors opened at the same time. Pull the handle the opposite direction and the cell doors all closed in unison. We immediately decided to become the prison guard and the criminal. An appropriate cell was chosen and then one of us would get in while the other pushed the handle and incarcerated his brother. We wondered excitedly how many bad guys had spent time in the cell and where they were now. We made a lot of noise, and looking back it seems strange that we were able to have the run of the building. The choice of trespassing into the old jailhouse seemed like a good idea to us, and we were soon facing another choice that also seemed like a great idea. While roaming around the building we came across the door of an old police car. It was from a 1956 Ford, painted cop car blue and, much to our excitement, still had the large police department badge painted on it. This was beyond cool and we both agreed that it needed to become our personal property.

We wanted that police car door but we faced one significant problem; we had arrived on a Lambretta motor scooter. The physics of both of us riding the scooter while hauling a police car door might be a bit challenging, but we agreed that we could figure out a method to successfully transport the car door to our home. What we were more concerned about was the visual impact on passersby as they noted two teenage boys traveling down the street on a motor scooter while lugging a car door that had previously been an essential part of a police car. We also gave some thought to the likelihood that any curious law enforcement officer might take offense to our acquisition of police property.

Our combined I.Q. of nearly three digits caused us to abandon the idea. We also gave some thought to what our father's reaction might be when he discovered the familiar looking police department property in one of his son's bedrooms.

I must admit that I've always regretted not attempting to bring home that beautiful blue door with the silver police badge painted on the side. I must also admit that back then, residing in the new jail for breaking into the old jail might have been the outcome. That door, however, would sure look great hanging in my garage today.

Shelley's Cycle Shop

What is six feet tall, mean looking and eats raw meat? Ol' Man Shelley!

Shelley was the owner of Shelley's Cycle Shop, one of several old businesses in the neighborhood where I grew up. In the 1950s and 1960s, many of the buildings that housed these businesses looked nearly identical to how they looked 100 years earlier. I frequently visited the establishment owned by Mr. Shelley because the product he sold was bicycles, accessories and bike repair.

Like most children, I became the owner of a bicycle at a young age. Unlike most children, I started at the top of the two-wheeled pecking order. My first bicycle was a Schwinn Black Phantom that was given to my father as payment for a debt. He gave it to me long before I was big enough to ride it. At the time I much preferred my sister's bike, despite it being a creepy girl's bike. It was fun to ride, and the lack of a center bar, like on all girls' bikes, made it possible for me to remain standing while pedaling. This was a good thing since I couldn't reach the pedals if I was sitting on the seat. I rode her bike until I was large enough to wrestle the heavy Phantom down the street.

Shelley's Cycle Shop was the only bicycle shop in my immediate neighborhood. It was a dark and dusty place that had bicycles everywhere. Bikes were lined up along the bare wood and warped floor, hanging from the ceiling and crowded into the window displays. Jesse Shelley purchased the shop in the early 1950s from Eugene Thomas, the person who had owned it since at least the early 1930s.

There were two older guys working there, one of whom was the stern Mr. Shelley. I remember that he did a lot of staring and not a lot of talking. He was shaped like a bowling pin, had the same amount of hair as a bowling pin, and was always dressed in bib overalls.

My occasional visits were always made cautiously because I didn't know if Mr. Shelley was going to say something pleasant or reach over the counter, grab me and eat me alive. On one visit he was standing behind the counter while holding a large piece of meat in one hand and a large knife in the other. I glanced at him and he stared back at me. Then he took the knife, cut a large slice of meat, reached across the counter and offered it to me. I saw this friendly gesture as more of a threat, so I declined his offer and avoided any further eye contact.

By the age of 14-years-old I'd become much too cool to be seen on a bicycle. I don't recall what happened to my Schwinn Black Phantom, other than it disappeared. At the age of 15-years-old I decided my *Tacoma News Tribune* newspaper route would be easier to deliver on a bicycle, so I put aside my childish pride and sought out another bike. I dug into my savings and headed for Shelley's Cycle Shop.

I did "own" a real car for a very brief period about this time. My father had given me a non-functioning and wheel-less 1949 Dodge. Within 24 hours I had sold it for $50 and added the money to my savings for a future car purchase. But for the time being it was going to be only two-wheeled transportation for me.

On display at Shelley's was a refurbished bicycle. It was painted (poorly) red and black. The condition was good and the price was very good -- fourteen dollars. I was a little embarrassed to be purchasing a bike at such an advanced age, but I wanted to cut down the time it took to deliver my paper route.

I put the cash in Mr. Shelley's meat-smelling hands and rode the bicycle home. I was excited about my new two-wheeled acquisition, but a bit worried that someone might see me riding a bicycle. Back then the only people on bicycles were children and teenagers who didn't have a car. I don't recall seeing an adult on a bicycle.

I pedaled the bike home and was greeted by my brother Lynn. He asked if he could take the bike for a ride, so I handed it over to him. This was a big mistake. He traveled one half of a block, decided to do a wheel-stand, leaned back and lifted the front wheel off of the ground. The front wheel then fell off of the bike. He panicked, hit the brakes and slammed the front de-wheeled forks into the sidewalk. The bike stopped, flipped over and cast my flailing sibling into the wind. The impact knocked him loopy, but no bones were broken. The bike, however, was badly damaged. The front fork looked like a pretzel.

Fixing the bike was an option, but I chose to toss it into a corner in the basement and forget about it. I took it as a message from above that I was not meant to have another bicycle, nor deliver my paper route rapidly. Eventually I moved on to my first hourly wage job and bought a car. I had no plans to ever own a bicycle again.

Shelley's Cycle Shop remained in business for many more years. Fortunately for Mr. Shelley, Schwinn Sting-Ray bikes and ten-speed English racing style bikes became very popular about the time I stopped riding bicycles.

As I write this there are five bicycles in my garden shed and one Schwinn Sting-Ray on display in my garage.

Bikes are cool.

Losers, Ladies and a Lambretta

I wasn't a hoodlum, but nearly everyone I ran around with was.

My first couple of years at Tacoma's Jason Lee (Chasing Fleas) Junior High School had been spent hanging out with the crowd that every parent hates -- the "bad kids". I felt that they were a lot more fun than the "good kids." They were, at least for a while. Then things began to get out of control. In the seventh grade we participated in activities and pranks that ranged from innocent to just a little bad. Perhaps definitions are in order. Innocent: jumping up and down of the rear bumper of grumpy Mr. Bass' 1956 Packard and making the suspension automatically raise the car. Just a little bad: sleeping overnight in a friend's back yard and swiping his parent's 1958 Nash and going for a joy ride. Not too serious stuff. Not yet anyway.

Then something happened in the summer of 1961. My buddies began removing parts off other people's cars rather than fooling around with the suspensions. (Did you know that only one screw holds the entire taillight assembly on a 1959 Cadillac?) Our crowd was now taking joy rides in cars whose owners we didn't know. What was a nice kid like me doing with this crowd of slammer-bound thugs?

I needed help.

I met Dale Query my first day in kindergarten and we have been good friends ever since. He was one of the "good kids" and, therefore, was not a part of the bad behavior of my immediate crowd. Dale came over one day and said that he wanted to talk to me "man to man". He had observed how things were getting out of hand with my crowd and that I needed to get away from them. He was right. He pointed out how some of my friends were juvenile delinquents who were headed for residence in state institutions. Again he was right. He reminded me that it didn't matter that I was not actually participating in the worst actions of the group. I would likely somehow get caught up in them and end up in jail with the rest of these guys. Yet again he was right. Then he said the magic words -- the words that almost every pubescent boy wants to hear: "I know a couple of girls that like you and think that you are cute." That was the good news. The bad news was that these girls would have nothing to do with me because I hung out with the "wrong crowd." I didn't need to hear any more. This was not a difficult choice: hang out with losers or hang out with a girl or two.

The change was overnight. I mean that literally. The next morning I began dressing differently, combing my hair differently and, most importantly, disassociating myself from the slammer-bound boys. I managed to quickly remove myself from this group; however, I still couldn't seem to get the attention of any of the promised girls. I needed a secret

weapon. Something that would make me the most irresistible boy in school. Something that would catapult me to the top of the desirable boy list. Something that no girl could resist. I needed a motor scooter!

My dad had recently purchased a brand new 150cc Lambretta motor scooter. No, it was not a fancy convertible or sexy sports car. What you have to remember is that these girls were 14 or 15 years old and any set of wheels impressed them, even if the set only included two wheels.

Here was my game plan: I would sneak out of school early, swipe dad's scooter and drive by the school just as the day's classes were ending. I sat parked a block away and waited as my fellow students spilled out onto the school yard and surrounding streets. I started the Lambretta and slowly passed by hundreds of my classmates. Many of them stopped and gaped at the kid on the scooter. I drove down the street, turned around and made another pass through the young crowd. My plan worked perfectly.

Jason Lee Junior High School

The following day classmates that had never spoken to me were now saying hello. Girls smiled at me as I passed down the school's hallways. I was receiving friendly stares rather than hostile glares. I didn't care that this acceptance was based on me having a vehicle. Anything that would open the right doors was OK with me.

Dear old Dad seemed to always look the other way when I would drop by his house (divorced parents, broken home, poor me) and borrow the Lambretta. His being a police officer resulted in other police officers not bothering the scooter-straddling squirt that was obviously too young to be driving.

I gave girls rides after school and was being invited to parties. "I'm having a party Saturday night and you are invited. Can you bring your scooter?" In a very short period I went from not being acknowledged by girls to having them sitting on the Lambretta with their arms around me and their bodies pressed against me.

Over the next year some significant things happened. A few members of my previous circle of friends ended up going to jail. Old grumpy Mr. Bass, who made his living as a beautician, became my mother's hairdresser. As I got a bit older he began showing up at my house to visit my mother. He'd toss me the keys to his 1955 Buick and tell me to go ahead and take it for a spin. The next thing I knew he was my stepfather. Illegally driving the Buick rather than the Lambretta seemed like a better choice.

I moved on to high school, bought a vehicle with four wheels, and fortunately maintained my place among the "good kids."

I still love Lambretta motor scooters.

Being a Cop's Kid

This book and others that I've previously written include stories that mention or focus on my father being a police officer for the City of Tacoma. To this day I am immensely proud of his choice of career.

My childhood friends' fathers had jobs that ranged from boring to moderately interesting. Dale's dad sold insurance, Jimmy's dad sold peanut butter and Dan's dad was a baker. Selling insurance seemed very dull, and being a baker didn't look like work to me. Selling peanut butter seemed like it would be very easy. Who can say no to peanut butter?

REX J. LAMBERT
Detective

TACOMA POLICE DEPARTMENT
County-City Building
Tacoma 2, Washington

FUlton 3-3311
Ext. 294

But being a police officer—now that was heroic! I, as the son of a police officer, was leading a life of privilege.

Probably the first thing apparent to me was how important and powerful Dad looked in his uniform. The dark blue slacks and light blue shirt blended together perfectly. The shiny black shoes looked regal and even a bit menacing. The black leather belt included various accessories necessary to catch and subdue members of Tacoma's underbelly. The handcuffs were held in a black leather pouch at the rear of the belt. At the front was another pouch filled with bullets to be used, at least in my imagination, during a shootout with one of America's 10 Most Wanted. And, of course, the most important item was the big gun on his hip. In my young mind I was sure he could pull it out faster than any cowboy on TV and twirl it in the air as he tossed it from hand to hand. He was a police officer, he was my father, and he could do anything!

"Sap" - a police officer's friend

In Dad's back pocket was something that fascinated me: his "sap" that was also called a "blackjack." He would occasionally let me hold and admire it as he would explain what it did and how he used it. It was shaped like the sole of a shoe, about 8 inches long, flat and bulbous at each end like the heel and toe areas of a shoe's sole. It contained a hunk of lead embedded between two thick pieces of stitched black leather. It was held at the small end of the "sole" and used to deliver attention-getting impacts to the heads of uncooperative arrestees.

"One or two whacks with this usually results in a person either being very cooperative or suddenly finding themselves taking an unexpected nap," Dad told me.

The most important thing, other than his gun, was the badge on his chest. This shiny piece of metal let the world know that he had the right to use the gun, handcuffs and sap as he saw fit. Fortunately, Dad was an easygoing guy and had a reputation for being gentle in his style of apprehension and arrest.

Frank, a longtime partner of his, once told me, "Your

dad came from a poor background and knew what it was like to be down and out. He knew that some of the people he was arresting were going through a tough time in their lives. He would talk to them in a way that made them realize he had some compassion for their situations."

The benefits of being a cop's kid were plentiful.

There were several movie theaters in downtown Tacoma, including the Roxy, Rialto and Music Box. Dad, along with other officers, was encouraged by theater managers to occasionally make an appearance. Seeing a uniformed police officer strolling through the lobby and down the aisles likely encouraged good behavior in otherwise possibly rambunctious teenagers. The managers showed their appreciation by giving my father an unlimited supply of movie passes for free admission to the theaters. Many a western saga and monster rampage were seen by the youngest Lambert as he sat for free in the front row of the Roxy.

Most of Tacoma's teenagers had to wait until the age of 16 to traverse the asphalt jungle while controlling a motor-powered vehicle. That was not the case for yours truly.

Previously described in this book and others was a two-wheeled Italian vehicle that brought unlimited fun to me and my friends, and all without the necessity of a driver's license. The town was small enough and the Lambretta motor scooter was distinctive enough for my father's co-workers to know that the skinny helmetless kid hanging onto the handlebars was Officer Lambert's youngest son. Upon sighting me they would choose to overlook my lack of legal documentation to be impeding traffic.

Reaching legal driving age and obtaining a driver's license still gave me a few opportunities to cash in on my father's occupation.

For example, on a few occasions some local law enforcement officials questioned my ability to properly operate a motor vehicle. Upon providing my driver's license I was usually asked one of two questions.

"Are you Rex Lambert's kid?" or "What does your father do for a living?"

More than once my confirmation that, "Yes, he is my father" or "He's a police officer, sir" resulted in my license being handed back to me with the comment, "Drive carefully young man, and have a good evening."

In other stories I've shared examples of the various items that ended up in our house as a result of Dad's occupation. I won't retell the stories, but know that more than once, the items that accompanied me to school were things not usually found in other kids' lockers. I was probably the only 6th grader with a switchblade knife sitting next to his sack lunch.

One evening when I was in the 3rd grade, Dad gathered my brother, sister and me around the kitchen table to show us something we knew very little about. He·reached into his shirt pocket and brought out something that looked vaguely familiar.

"Kids, this is a marijuana cigarette. It is a drug and you should never smoke it."

To me it looked like a cigarette that had been out in the rain. It was lumpy, brownish in color and looked like it had been stepped on, and that is how I described it at my class Show & Tell the next day. I'm confident that this was likely the first time a student had described their experience with drugs to their classmates at Franklin Elementary School.

There were times when being a cop's kid had a dark side.

Many Christmases were spent with the family roster incomplete because Officer Lambert was required to help keep the cold and empty streets of Tacoma safe from any recklessly driving and high flying red-nosed reindeer.

The City of Tacoma was notorious for having one of the lowest paying police departments in the nation. Many officers, including my father, had to take on a second job to pay the family bills.

Dad attempted to be a successful Kirby vacuum cleaner salesman as well as selling life insurance. I do not recall any Salesman-of-the-Month awards hanging on our living room wall.

Another bad employment practice by the City Government was the requirement for police officers to work various shifts. The officers were required to work two months on the day shift, then two months on the night shift and then two months on the graveyard shift. The result was that they were always tired. Dad was a good-natured guy who was always smiling, but many days we were told, "Keep your voice down, your father is sleeping."

Perhaps the worst part of being a police officer was the potential danger they faced and the difficult situations they needed to deal with.

On one occasion I remember being told by our mother that my siblings and I needed to be good and not upset our father. Earlier that day he had had to deal with a traffic-related death and the situation and circumstances had been very tough for him. We were cautious and within a few days his great smile returned.

My pride in his occupation was bolstered on one occasion when his actions resulted in his picture being on the front page of the *Tacoma News Tribune*.

The Safeway grocery store, located on the corner of North 6th & Pine, was robbed by a lone gunman. My father was the first on the scene and he pulled out his gun, pointed it at the robber and told him to get on the ground. The robber instead decided to run. Officer Lambert, rather than shoot, holstered his pistol and chased after the culprit. Dad caught up with the robber, tackled him and placed him under arrest. The newspaper lauded his decision to not shoot and hailed him as a hero. Once again Dad's badge and honor shone bright in my eyes.

I do not intend to portray my father as a perfect example of a parent. He had his failings, for which I judged him harshly, as young people always do, and there were times when our relationship was strained. He and my mother had divorced, and for several years Dad and I went our separate ways.

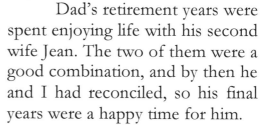

Dad's retirement years were spent enjoying life with his second wife Jean. The two of them were a good combination, and by then he and I had reconciled, so his final years were a happy time for him.

My brother and I had the good fortune to spend some of his final days at his side, and I'll never forget the pride he took in introducing us to the staff at the hospital. While he was there I gave him a teddy bear that was dressed in a police uniform. He seemed to love it and was holding it the last time I saw him. A few days later he went home from the hospital, and not long afterwards he passed away. His wife Jean said that the teddy bear was at his side when Officer Lambert left this world.

Armory Impression

Old cars, rock & roll music and a building that looks like a castle—what do these three things have to do with each other? Let me explain:

Hot rod and custom car clubs in Tacoma were a big thing when I was growing up. To my crowd, anyone who was a member of the Toppers, Drag-Ons, Capers, Rickshaws, Demonos, Stompers and a few other clubs was someone to be looked up to. These clubs were made up of the coolest guys in town; you could tell by the club jackets they wore and the club plaques that were displayed on their cars. They were selective in who they allowed in their clubs, and the member's cars were usually fast and great looking.

Fabulous Wailers

The music scene in Tacoma was also a source of pride. There were many bands and many dances, and at the top of the pecking order was the Fabulous Wailers, or to most people, just the Wailers. Many of the bands in Washington, Oregon and Idaho admitted to being Wailers "wannabees" and proved it by including most of the Wailers original music in their playlists. The band deserved the accolades and they assured their local status when they recorded the #1 hit record, "Tall Cool One," in 1959. Their fans in the Northwest were filled with pride when the Wailers appeared on Dick Clark's *American Bandstand* show.

The Wailers appearing on "American Bandstand"

Another source of pride for the residents of *The City of Destiny* was the National Guard Armory. This enormous structure was built in 1908 and featured an architectural design that resembled a British castle.

So what do you get when you combine car clubs, rock & roll music and a building that looks like a castle? The answer: you get one of the most impressive experiences in my life.

When I was growing up indoor custom car shows

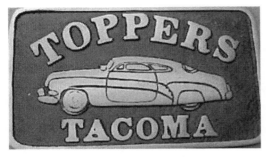

were a rare occurrence in Tacoma, and in 1959 I was lucky enough to attend one of the most impressive of them all. The show was put on by the Toppers Car Club (founded in 1951 as the Tacoma Toppers Car Club, but always referred to as just the Toppers by everyone I knew) and was held at the National Guard Armory (aka Tacoma Armory). The local rock & roll radio station was advertising the show, and there was a promotional poster in the window of the hobby shop where I purchased one AMT model car each month with my newspaper delivery money.

I heard the advertisement and saw the poster, so there was no stopping me from going to the show.

When the weekend of the show arrived, I dipped into my cigar box safe and removed the necessary 75 cents entry fee, walked one block to my friend Dan's house, and then he and I walked the one mile to the car show.

Approaching the Armory in itself was exciting. I'd seen it many times because it was so close to my home, but each time I was equally impressed. It would have been appropriate to see Sir Lancelot and the Knights of the Roundtable standing guard at the top of the corner turrets. The brick structure was huge to my young eyes, and my imagination was always on high alert when I was near the building.

Now, visualize that building full of the best customs and hot rods from up and down the West Coast. I was prepared to be impressed, but I was not prepared for what I was about to see.

I walked up the ramp and entered the huge castle-like entry doors. Directly in front of me was one of the most

Tacoma's National Guard Armory

famous cars in the Northwest, a 1927 Ford roadster pickup. This beauty was built and owned by the Toppers Car Club, and was considered, at least by me and all my car loving friends, to be as cool as a custom car could be. I thought this moment could not get better, but it did.

Toppers' 1927 T-Bucket Ford

As I was admiring the Ford a drumbeat began filling the hall, accompanied by two guitars, saxophone, piano and an organ. There, beyond the bright colored and sparkling sea of hot rods and custom cars was the Wailers on stage! I did not know they were going to be performing at the show. The moment that I entered the Armory, saw the Toppers show car and heard Tacoma's best band was overwhelming.

Dan and I spent the next several hours gaping at the cars, swaying spellbound in front of the bandstand, and then exiting the glorious Armory as we excitedly shared opinions on what were the best cars on display and what were the best songs performed by the Wailers.

I began my transition from small plastic model cars to full-sized metal cars a few years after that impressive Saturday. My appreciation for the Wailers continued and in 1966 I went on the road with the band as one of their roadies, or "band boys" as we were known as back then. My appreciation for the Armory also continued, and recently I talked to a local promoter about the possibility of hosting a car show in the structure. Yes, the Wailers are still performing, there are a few members of the Toppers Car Club still around and the Armory is available to rent. But if I do sponsor a car show there, I'll have a hard time topping the experience I had more than 50 years ago.

My First Car Club

I've had two great passions since I was old enough to push a toy car on the kitchen floor -- automobiles and clubs. By the time I was 12 years old I had started the Junior Fireman Club, the Junior G-Man Club, the Back Alley Boys and the Oddballs.

When I was 14 years old I wanted to join the Toppers Car Club. They were the most active and respected club in the town. I was allowed to attend several of their meetings; however, they said I couldn't join until I was 16 years old and had a driver's license. They did offer to help me start the "Junior" Toppers Car Club. I felt that I was beyond the "junior" stage so I stopped attending Toppers meetings and started my own club.

Most of my closest friends were into cars as much as I was, so I recruited them to become charter members. There were five of us, aged 15 and 16, with two members owning cars. Bob Dillon had a 1947 Hudson and Greg Eling had a 1940 Chevrolet. It was the summer of 1962 and there we were, Greg Eling, Bob Dillon, Doug Sparks, Dale Query and me, sitting in my parent's garage. First of all we had to come up with a name for the club. I picked up an old copy of "Ivanhoe" and started glancing at pages to see if anything jumped out at me. I saw the word *steeds* and that was it! Steeds equaled horsepower and strength. It was perfect. We agreed on the name and began the next steps in organizing a club -- designing the club's emblem, car club plaques membership card and club courtesy card. It soon became apparent that a better club name could have been chosen. People occasionally asked "Steve's car club? Who's Steve?' or "Why a horse? Is this a 4H club?"

15 year old Lance and his new Steeds Car Club jacket

Our first emblem featured a T-bucket hot rod but we soon changed that to a more fitting horse's head and engine combination.

We quickly overcame any name-related problems and become one of the largest and most active car clubs in town. We had what I considered the best looking jackets of any of the clubs, several car-show-winning vehicles, a club dragster (later destroyed by flying off of the trailer and crashing into the tow truck), and memberships in the International Car Club Association and the Northwest Car Club Council. At any given time there were usually about 15 active members in our club.

The member's cars ranged from beater four-door sedans to a new Corvette. Some members, like me, were happy with cars that would get them reliably from home to the local drive-in and back again. Others were only content when they felt their car was the fastest on the boulevard. My contributions to the club's roster were a mildly customized two-door 1948 Chevrolet Fleetline and a lowered and rumbling 1954 Oldsmobile 88 two-door hardtop. The Fleetline had a lowered front end and a partially rolled and pleated interior. The Oldsmobile was lowered three inches, had a leaded-in trunk lid and chrome reversed front wheels. Of course each car proudly displayed the club plaque in the rear window.

The majority of my attention during my high school years was divided between the club and my girlfriend. I couldn't wait for the next kiss from Kayleen

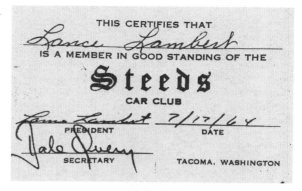

or the next weekly club meeting. She often accused me of caring more for the club and my car than I did for her. I was smart enough to change the subject when it came up.

I graduated from high school and prepared to travel to Hawaii and attend college. I reluctantly had to sell my car and my club jacket before leaving fore school.

Courtesy card

When I returned home I was pleased to find that the club was still very active, but one concern was that the membership consisted of a bunch of younger guys that I didn't know. Another thing that bothered me was that they didn't seem to be impressed that I was one of the original founding members. It didn't really matter because I'd moved to Seattle and began my VW driving hippy days.

The times were changing.

Club jacket and logo

Club plaque design from '62 until early '70s

Second club plaque design used until the late '70s

Popularity Pressure

A student entering the first year of high school faces many pressures. Some are legitimate and some—like those in the story I'm about to tell—are self-inflicted.

During my first few weeks at Stadium High School I allowed myself to be overcome with the fear of not being accepted by my new classmates. I wanted more than anything to be one of the "popular" students. The rungs on the ladder to popularity were climbed in various ways and one surefire way to jump a few rungs, at least in my opinion, was to become a member of one of the "social clubs" on campus. These clubs were high school versions of fraternities and sororities and, like real fraternities and sororities, assured the members a place high on the social ladder at the school, or at least that is what I thought. There were many classmates who had a different opinion of these organizations, but for me, belonging to a social club was very important.

There were several clubs for boys, including the Royals, Bengals, Stasons and Lancers. The clubs included students from both Stadium High School and nearby Wilson High School. Wilson was Stadium's friendly rival because many of the students in both schools grew up together and remained good friends even when they ended up at different high schools. The name Stasons was created by combining *Sta* from *Sta*dium and *sons* from Wil*son*.

So there I was in a new school filled with many

longtime friends and a larger number of students I'd never met before. How hard was it going to be getting accepted by these strangers and becoming someone they considered a friend? I was 15 years old and these were very important questions. I'd heard about the social clubs and it seemed that belonging to one would quickly create a new circle of friends. The challenge was how to become a member. A student had to be asked to join by someone that was already a member. All I could do was wait and hope that an invitation would come my way.

Stadium High School

These clubs were definitely *not* approved by the school authorities. They were greatly frowned upon and students were discouraged from joining or participating in any club's activities. This, of course, made membership even more desirable.

The Royals were considered the coolest club, and within a few weeks several of my good friends were asked to become pledges in this group. Like fraternities, potential members had to be offered membership, go through a pledge period that included hazing, and then be voted upon for membership. I was happy for them and nervously waited to be invited to join the Royals. That invitation never arrived.

I had all the maturity of a 15 year old and was absolutely sure that I'd be a social outcast throughout my high school years if I didn't become a member of a social club. The period of recruiting pledges was nearly over and I began to accept the possibility that I'd frequently be answering the question, "What club are you in?" with a mumbled response of, "None" or the lie, "I chose not to belong to a club."

At the time I was very active in the Steeds Car Club, but that was a different thing and it didn't carry the same social status as did the school-related clubs. Membership in a car club was cool to car guys but meant very little to anyone who did not have an interest in cars.

Lancers club pin

I was beginning to accept my likely clubless fate when the clouds parted and the rays of possible acceptance shone upon me. A member of the Lancers asked if I'd be interested in pledging. What a perfect club for a guy named Lance! The Lancers, Stasons and Bengals were all Royals wannabes but they were better than not being in any club. I was extremely grateful, immediately accepted the invitation and looked forward to my first meeting.

The process of becoming a member included a pledge period with requirements ranging from humorous to embarrassing, and hazing that ranged from mild to mean.

Lancer members and prospective members, as well as members of the other clubs, wore white shirts and skinny black ties to school on Wednesdays. This looked sharp and also identified you as a participant in the pseudo fraternity community. Some of our fellow students were impressed by our appearance and others were, perhaps, embarrassed for us.

Various requirements were placed upon the pledges. One that still makes me laugh today is when I was told by a member that I could not turn right anytime while walking in school that day. If I needed to go to the right then I had to make a continuous left turn until I was facing the direction I needed to go. I looked very silly spinning around in the halls and classrooms.

Another requirement placed upon me was cleaning Stan Topolski's garage. I would have done most anything to get out of cleaning my own family's garage, but cleaning Stan's was acceptable for two reasons: it would likely help get me into the Lancers and it might also help me get to know his good looking sister Lydia. I was partially successful. It did help the membership efforts, but unfortunately, it did little to endear me to Lydia.

The hazing activity was a bit harsher, however, than left turns and garage cleaning.

The Lancers met every Wednesday evening, and during the pledge period each meeting ended with the prospective members getting hacks. Hacks consisted of a healthy teenage boy vigorously swinging a paddle through the air until it made swift and direct contact with the buttocks of a prospective member. This was repeated several times and, like so many things in life, was endured by the recipient and enjoyed by the administrator.

This may be the appropriate time to ask the question, "Why?" Why would anyone allow their lower cheeks to become radiant red and super sore when it was totally avoidable? A better question might be why did I allow myself to be hit with a paddle? It all goes back to the pressure of wanting to be accepted and believing that the ticket to being in the "in crowd" was being part of the club crowd. What better way is there to accomplish this goal than to let a bunch of young guys, most of whom I barely knew, beat me with a large piece of wood?

Lancers club beer stein

The pledging period lasted about three or four weeks before the decision was to be made about my acceptance into the Lancers. Ron Gardner was a full-fledged member and a local rock & roll star who a few years later became a member of the Wailers. He called me on a Wednesday after school and said, "Put up with anything tonight. You are probably going to get in." Finally, I was assured of popularity!

I left home early that evening slightly confident that my goal was going to be accomplished. The meeting was held at a member's home, and as the official part of the gathering was completed the hazing portion began. On that evening there were only two pledges in attendance: Chuck

Heinz and me. Jack Hart, president of the Lancers, looked at the two of us and said, "We have made something special for you to eat. Whichever of you finishes eating it first will not get hacks tonight."

The concoction we were consuming was made up from a large variety of ingredients found in the kitchen. Hopefully nothing in the mix came from the bathroom. The gloppy mess was spread upon two pieces of bread and one slice was handed to me and the other slice to Chuck. Jack told us to begin our meal and we obediently obliged. The good news is that I completed eating my deli delight first.

Then came the bad news. Jack, dressed in the mandatory white shirt and skinny black tie, was standing about two feet in front of me. He stood there watching me doing my best to keep the Mr. Yuk open-faced sandwich down. His close proximity to me was a bad choice on his part. What I had successfully consumed was now being rejected by my stomach and was beginning its return trip back up my tummy's turnpike. Jack remained standing there as I looked at him, opened my mouth and expelled the contents of my stomach onto his no-longer-white shirt and black tie.

Jack was a cool guy and always carried himself with an air of dignity. The barf banquet landing on his chest did not seem to faze him at all. He did not jump back, get angry or even laugh. He just casually looked down at the mess, looked back up at me and said ever so calmly, "You're in."

I stood there with puke on my chin, down my chest and on the floor between Jack and me. It didn't matter because I broke out in a huge smile upon realizing that the Lancers had accepted me as a member.

As the sophomore year passed my participation and interest in the Lancers began to wane. The self-inflicted pressure to be popular diminished as I realized that acceptance came by just being me and accepting others for who they were, regardless of whether or not they belonged to any club or organization.

I don't know if I was "popular," but I do know that I was blessed with many wonderful friends, many who are still close friends today.

'Gators in the Gym

For many of us high school dances were a big part of our teenage years. For me an evening of scuffing up the gymnasium floor was usually fun, sometimes embarrassing and, on at least one occasion, a dismal failure.

Dances at Stadium High School were frequent, well attended and usually successful. The money raised through the ticket admission price was always directed to a school club or class treasury, to be used for the purchase of some item needed by the students of the school.

Part of the fun was the preparation for the dances. A dance committee was created, a rock & roll band was booked, posters were hand painted and hung in the halls, and occasionally tickets were sold in advance.

I was the head of the committee for one dance that was raising money for supplies to be used in the school's Distributive Education class. D.E., as it was referred to by the students, was a class that attempted to teach business skills to future entrepreneurs. I did a good job of organizing everything needed for the dance, but a bad job of choosing the band to provide the music.

There was one band that, if hired to play, assured without question a successful dance. The Galaxies were popular for a good reason: they were great. The most popular bands in Tacoma were the Wailers and the Sonics, both of which were too expensive for most high school dance budgets. The Galaxies were considered the "affordable

173

Wailers" and, as a result, were busy playing dances all over town. Eventually they recorded on the Wailers label, *Etiquette*, as did the Sonics.

The mistake I made was not booking the Galaxies. A good friend was the drummer in another band and I decided, due to nepotism and poor judgment, to hire his band. Big mistake! To the band's credit they were playing music that was less traditional rock & roll and, instead, more reflective of some of the changing styles that were happening in the music scene at that time. The problem was the students didn't attend the dances to advance their knowledge of the changing style of music. They were there to dance to popular rock & roll songs that they were familiar with. The only thing dancing on the gymnasium floor that evening were the tumbleweeds blowing across the surface. Thanks to me the D.E. class lost money on that failed business venture. Fortunately, I'm still friends with the drummer, despite the fact that there was no money to pay the band that night so many years ago. The good news for him is that several years later he became the drummer for the Galaxies.

The Galaxies – Stuart Turner, Mark Eubanks, Phil Hanson, Bob Koch, Rob Lowery, Chuck Naubert

For many high schools the "Homecoming" event was a big deal. A Homecoming Queen, Princess and Duchess were chosen and they, as stated in my 1965 Stadium yearbook, were, "Stadium Royalty reigning during Homecoming Week..." My high school sweetheart Kayleen was chosen as the Homecoming Princess, and for her and the other royalty, "... the coronation took place at the fun-filled dance which climaxed the seven-day celebration to welcome home former Stadium students."

The dance was well attended by the students. The "coronation" consisted of Kayleen, along with the "Duchess" and "Queen," walking up to the stage in the gymnasium to be crowned. It was similar to bridesmaids and a bride walking down the aisle with the guests standing on either side of the procession. The young ladies were to be escorted by a suit-wearing fellow student and, for whatever reason, Kayleen's escort was nowhere to be found. I had not been happy that she was being escorted by someone other than me, so the absence of her designated escort came as good news. I stepped up and announced that I'd be happy to do the honors. There was only one problem: I was not wearing a suit and my continental slacks and madras shirt, though pretty darn spiffy, were not acceptable. What was I to do?

This was a moment for quick thinking. There was not enough time for me to get home and put on my own suit. My buddy Darrol was standing next to me and, since he lived two blocks from the school, I asked, "Do you have a suit I can wear?" Darrol was larger than I was, but his brother Dick was about the same size, or so we thought. We raced out the door, ran to Darrol's house and raided his brother's closet.

I changed into the suit and necessary accoutrements and realized that Dick, like Darrol, was also larger than I was. There was no "Plan B," so I tightened up the belt, puffed out my chest and did my best not to look like a baseball in a basketball net. We hurried back to the gymnasium and reported to the Homecoming authorities. I think they, along with Kayleen, took a look at me and decided that Mr. Baggypants was better than nothing, so the procession commenced.

The individual members of the Homecoming royalty were announced and, as the names were called, we began our walk down the aisle to the stage. I felt a little awkward in the borrowed baggy attire, but that was offset by the feeling that the Homecoming Princess was holding the arm of the appropriate escort. We reached the stage, Kayleen took her spot and I stepped off to the side. At that moment I was very proud of her and did not care about the oversized suit. I took the Princess home, returned the baggy suit and my escort duties were completed.

There were many popular dance styles in the 1960s, including the Stroll, Twist, Mashed Potato, Jerk, Limbo and several more. Many did not last any longer than the hit song that described the dance to the listening audience. There was one style of "dancing," however, that had a special distinction. It was known as the Gator. This consisted of a few preliminary movements done while standing, quickly followed by dropping to the ground and flopping around in a style that appeared to be a combination of pushups, exercise burpees, fornication and trying to get a swarm of bees out of your pants. John Belushi and his fraternity brothers did a version of the Gator in the movie *Animal House*. I do not recall ever seeing a female do the Gator. All of the practitioners in my crowd were guys and we all thought this formalized floor flopping was the height of dance prowess. We may have been in a minority.

What was distinctive about the Gator was that doing it guaranteed the practitioner immediate expulsion from the dance. For that reason it was only done under certain circumstances: you attended the dance without a date; you'd been drinking in the parking lot before the dance; one of your least liked teachers was standing near; the dance was almost over; the dance chairman had hired a band other than the Galaxies and you planned on leaving the dance early anyway.

The chaperones were not pleased when they saw you hit the boards, flop around and appear to be attempting to make a baby with the gymnasium floor, and they would be on you like coffee stains on a teacher's tie. Gator gyrators didn't get a second chance. The evening's authority figure would assist you up from the floor with one hand and point to the exit door with the other. This was usually met with approval from the dancer's classmates, but I was smart enough never to Gator in the presence of the Homecoming Princess. She would have directed me to the exit door from the dance and the exit door from her life.

———

The last high school dance I attended was the Senior Prom. Kayleen and I were no longer dating, so the search was on for someone else to accompany me to what many teenagers are brainwashed into believing is one of life's most important events. I had a mild interest in a certain classmate and thought asking her to the prom would be a good place to start. She turned me down and, instead, she asked someone else if he would go to the prom with her. A couple of years later her prom date became the first person I knew who was sentenced to a few years in a federal prison.

I had recently met a young lady from another high school. She had a lifeless personality but a gorgeous face and carriage. I thought that an evening with me would completely change her into the most magnetic person at the dance. I was wrong. It's still a mystery why she agreed to be my date. We barely knew each other and the dance was not even at her school. Maybe her mother liked me and made her accept the invitation.

1962 Thunderbird

The silver lining to the evening was borrowing my stepfather's 1962 Thunderbird convertible. It was "Chalfonte Blue" with a white top and interior. I envisioned an evening that started with me arriving at my beautiful date's door, helping her into the flashy convertible, arriving at the prom, being admired and envied by all within sight, and dancing the night away as I transformed my date from a pretty face with little to say into the most popular belle of the ball.

The evening was a failure on all accounts, with the exception of being able to drive the convertible. She didn't want to dance. She didn't want to talk. She didn't want to meet any of my friends. Our evening together was a contender for the worst date of my life, including all dates prior to or after that night.

I think she may have been wondering what she was doing at another school's senior prom with a guy she hardly knew. We agreed to leave early and drove quietly back to her home. I was a gentleman so I must have walked her to the door. Most likely there was an awkward goodbye, no kiss, and a quick retreat to the convertible. I never called her again. I picked up the prom photographs when the school made them available and immediately threw them into a trash can.

The limited interest in and practice of dancing that I had was based almost entirely on pursuing members of the opposite sex. I do not ever recall saying to any high school friend, "Gee, I feel like dancing tonight!" I may have said, "Let's go to the dance tonight and see what girls are there." Whatever the motivation was, the memories of dances in the Stadium High School's gym bring a smile to my face.

The Cool Guy

"Coolness is an aesthetic of attitude, behavior, comportment, appearance and style which is generally admired... It has associations of composure and self-control and is often used as an expression of admiration or approval... One consistent aspect is that cool is widely seen as positive and desirable." Wikipedia.com

There were two or three in every school: the teenage versions of Steve McQueen walking the school halls, or James Dean hanging out in the parking lot. He was the Paul Newman that came across as both friendly and fearless, or the Sean Connery type casually glancing at the girls, knowing that any one of them would respond positively to an offer of a ride home, or an invitation to the next school dance.

You wanted him to be your friend but knew that he was selective in his choice of colleagues. The lucky among us would occasionally receive a nod or smile from him. The blessed were actually spoken to and perhaps even accepted as a friend.

Who was this guy who carried himself with a quiet confidence that let you know he expected to be respected, and whose smile made you feel important and whose glare sent a chill up and down your spine? His walk displayed just enough bravado to let everyone know that he was not to be trifled with, but he was also the guy the girls always shyly smiled at when he walked by.

He was *The Cool Guy.*

There were a few guys of this type at Stadium High School, but only one of them stood out as the best example of what many teenage boys aspired to be, or at least what I wished I'd become by this time early in my life.

His name was Chuck Naubert.

Chuck had it all going for him. He was movie star handsome, physically fit and oozed personal magnetism. He walked the halls with a slight smile/smirk similar to that of Elvis. Classmates looked his way in the hope of a salutation. The boys knew Chuck's acknowledgment would help their status, and the girls hoped that a smile might be followed by a few moments of his attention. Chuck had his choice of female companionship, but chose to be the boyfriend of one of the school's most revered cheerleaders.

The friends I had in school were plentiful, and the number of close friends sufficient that a buddy or two were always around to accompany me on various adventures. We were respected by our fellow students and, most of the time, didn't have any trouble finding a date for the weekend or a girlfriend for more permanent companionship. We were happy and usually ended each day with a reasonable amount of satisfaction. We were *entry level cool*, but we were not *Chuck Naubert cool.*

What else was Chuck packing in his cool guy cache?

How about being a local rock & roll star? Chuck was a founding member and bass player for the Galaxies, one of the most popular bands in Tacoma. They were only surpassed in popularity by the Wailers and the Sonics.

In addition to plunking the strings of a bass guitar he also stroked the strings of a cello in the school's orchestra. For some people cello playing does not leap to mind when thinking of what is cool. The rules changed when the Rubenesque instrument found its way onto the stage with Chuck. Many high school dance attendees were confused when they looked up to see the Galaxies' bass player put down his guitar and prop up his cello. When the song started the doubt stopped. He made the audience wonder why every rock & roll band didn't include a cello player scrubbing the catgut.

What did Chuck use for transportation? Most of us drove anything we could afford. This often meant a rattling and rusty Ford or Chevy purchased for $50 to $75. Chuck cruised 6th Avenue, Tacoma's north end equivalent to the cruising streets seen in *American Graffiti*, in a dignified 1946 Cadillac Coupe de Ville.

Chuck and his 1946 Cadillac parked by Stadium High School

The cheerleader referred to was considered by several classmates to be *THE* cheerleader. Sue Elrod was a pretty brunette whom I considered Stadium High School's answer to Annette Funicello, the Disney Mouseketeer, actress and recording artist. My buddies and I discreetly watched her walk down the school's hallways. Sometimes our view was obscured by the dark-haired guy who was carrying her books.

The cheerleaders were chosen by a vote from the students, and the finalists performed at an assembly where votes were cast to decide who would be on the cheerleading squad. One year Sue broke her arm prior to the final performance and, although she participated, she could not perform many of the expected cheers. It didn't matter, she was still voted in as a cheerleader. There may have been one or two students, perhaps more, who attended the school's athletic events to watch her rather than watch the actual play on the court or field.

It is likely that every school had its own version of Chuck Naubert. It is also likely that my opinion was not held by all of the other students at Stadium. A classmate may read this story and feel that another student was more worthy of the title of *The Cool Guy*. As the cliché goes, *To each his own.*

The days spent at Stadium High School eventually became part of the various students' past history. No matter if we were cool or not, the next phase of our lives was opening before us. Some chose to continue their education or serve in the military. Others entered the workforce or stayed home to raise children.

What became of *cool guy* Chuck Naubert? He and his high school sweetheart Sue Elrod got married and raised a family. Did Chuck, like so many former *cool guys* of the world, end up just another guy selling wholesale plumbing parts or managing a grocery store? No, the coolness never left.

Chuck went on to have a career as a commercial airline pilot.

Frisko Freeze and Friends

Most everyone's youth included a favorite hangout; perhaps it was the corner drugstore, gas station or a favorite restaurant. During my crowd's high school years the place to be was Frisko Freeze. It was a typical '50s and '60s style small drive-in that sold the expected hamburgers, fries, shakes and other foods that current-day nutritionists have deemed somewhere between unhealthy and highly toxic. Back then we didn't care and could not get enough of the greasy calories handed to us through the drive-up window.

The 1973 movie *American Graffiti* did a great job of displaying a slightly romanticized depiction of 1962 teenage life in the parking lot of Mel's Drive-In. The asphalt area of Frisko Freeze was much smaller, and there was no indoor seating, but for all of the patrons it was just as important to them as Mel's was to any of the characters in the movie.

My friends referred to our hangout as "The Freeze" and we were there several times during the week and nearly every Friday and Saturday evening. Stadium High School dances and sporting events were usually followed with a visit to Frisko Freeze, and many non-diet Cokes and grease soaked bags of fries were bought during the week on our way home from school.

Despite food being served, that was not the top priority for a visit. The list, starting from the top, went like this: socializing, flirting, showing off your car, getting something to eat, and last but importantly, either getting into or not getting into a fight.

The socializing was easy because there were always friends hanging out. On a good night several of my buddies would wave hello as I arrived in my 1948 Chevrolet or 1954 Oldsmobile and pulled into the parking lot or parked out on the street. We'd gather in groups, laugh, brag, tease each other and make plans for the evening or weekend. On weekend evenings we might spread the news about a party or some other social event, and at other times the socializing in the parking lot was the party of the evening.

The majority of the parking lot population was male, but there were always a few cars with one to five young ladies cruising across the tarmac. Usually they were friends, or maybe one in particular was a girl that I wanted to become friends with. I guess Frisko Freeze was our pre-computer era dating site. It was also a great place for me to learn that females could also become friends, and not just someone that I wanted to date. The parking lot also provided a place to sit in my car and show off my pretty girlfriend, or when I didn't have a girlfriend, find a girl that was willing to share a kiss between sharing bites of burgers and sips of soda.

The evening's pecking order was usually determined by which guy arrived in the coolest car. My Chev and Olds were somewhere near the middle of the acceptable pack so I could park with a reasonable amount of pride. At the top were guys like Bob Mitchell behind the wheel of his beautiful 1948 Chev or Doug Sparks in his 1961 Oldsmobile. Hovering at the bottom of the list was Dave Daily in his 1958 Renault Dauphine, or any guy in his parent's four-door sedan of any manufacturer.

435   GOOD FOR
ONE BURGER & SHAKE
AT
FRISKO FREEZE
DRIVE-IN
1201 DIVISION AVENUE   TACOMA, WASHINGTON
"HOME OF THE BEEFBURGER"
QUARTS   PINTS   CONES   SUNDAES
FRIES   COLD DRINKS AND COFFEE
FOR PICK-UP ORDERS CALL BR 2-6843

One of my proudest moments was arriving, parking and coolly walking away from my Oldsmobile as it's new chrome rims reflected the neon glow of the Frisko Freeze sign. I could only afford two of these glistening wheels on the front, but back then chrome wheels only on the front and black rims on the back meant that you had a fast car and were obviously drag-racing it and had to have special wheels and tires on the rear.

The prices have increased but the lettering has stayed the same

Food was not always a priority, much to the frustration of the management. The owner, Perry Smith, occasionally called the police to rid the parking lot of the deadbeats taking up space but not buying food. Word would spread quickly that the cops were in route, so my cash strapped friends and I would buy one of the two cheapest items on the menu, a small Coke or a bag of popcorn. This was enough to keep the law away and placate Perry.

There were occasionally fights in the parking lot. I managed to get through my academic years with only a couple of minor skirmishes, but there were a few memorable battles fought by others at The Freeze. My friend Loren Ezell taking on three soldiers from nearby Fort Lewis made a lasting impression on his classmates and even more of an impression on the face of one soldier. My sense of survival always kicked-in before trouble started, causing me to either leave the area or keep plenty of distance between me and anyone seeking somebody's face to bloody his knuckles on.

Most of the teenagers arriving were known or recognized by the regular patrons. They were either from Stadium High School, or from our friendly rival, Wilson High School. Many of us had grown up with "Wilsonites" and were still good friends with them. The rival high school that was not friendly was Lincoln High School. A car full of unknown individuals often began its trek from the south-end of Tacoma where the Lincoln students resided. Usually they stayed in their cars, but climbing out of a car and staring too long at the wrong Stadium student could start a fight.

I made my first visit to Frisko Freeze when I was in the ninth grade and it didn't take long for someone to single me out and challenge me to a fight. My brother has helped me out in life at various times and he rescued me on this particular Saturday afternoon. What was interesting is that he was not even there. As I was being verbally assaulted I heard someone call out to the assailant, "Leave him alone. He's Lambert's brother." The guy stopped "giving me lip" and walked away. Thanks again Lynn!

The amazing thing about Frisko Freeze is that it has not changed since I was hanging out there over 50 years ago. The building, signs and parking lot are exactly the same. The paint is touched up when necessary, electric light bulbs and neon replaced when needed in the signs, and the parking lot is re-striped when wheels and weather takes a toll.

I still dine at Frisko Freeze one or two times a year, always with a lifelong friend that was there with me when we were in high school.

The fries and friendship are just as good now as they were back then.

Beer Bowl 500

It was late on a Saturday evening in 1964, the stadium was empty and Sandy's go-kart was the only vehicle on the track. It was a perfect evening for teenage boys to create a memory.

Sandy was the type of guy everybody loved. He was funny, friendly, generous, supportive and always there when a friend needed a friend. His unique living situation also added to his appeal. His family owned, operated and lived in a very small neighborhood grocery store. It was a charming building resembling something you'd expect to see in a Norman Rockwell painting.

Sandy, like all of his close friends, was nuts about anything with a motor and wheels. The store's basement held a huge slot-car track built by Sandy and his friends. Every horizontal surface in his bedroom was covered with greasy used car parts and even his bed didn't escape the horizontal hosting of parts. He used one half of the bed to store car parts and the other half for sleeping.

Sandy's cars, or at least the remnants of cars, consisted of a 1948 Plymouth and a 1949 Chevrolet with a collapsed roof. None of these cars held our interest on this particular summer's evening. What did was his go-kart. In our crowd owning a go-kart was equal to owning the most desirable toy available on the face of the earth. The difficult part was where to safely drive the go-kart.

Tacoma's Stadium High School (also known as "The Castle" due to its architectural design), was our academic prison during the school year. It was located exactly one block away from Sandy's home. Immediately north of the school was a large sports stadium known as the Stadium Bowl. The Stadium Bowl was just that, a huge subterranean bowl where sporting and civic events had been held regularly since 1910. Fortunately on this particular summer evening it was unused and empty with the exception of Sandy, Bob, Darrol and me. Off to the bowl we went with the go-kart and several recently procured beers. We were all 17 years old and, therefore, an evening of sharing beers and driving the go-kart promised to be both a memorable and an illegal event. Technically we were committing a few crimes, but drinking a beer and driving the go-kart around the bowl seemed quite innocent.

The "Beer Bowl 500" race drivers were the best of friends. We had begun hanging out together while attending Jason Lee Junior High School and had originally become friends because of our shared love of cars. Sandy was an excellent artist and drew pictures of cars for his friends. Bob was my first close friend to have a driver's license and he was the proud owner of a 1947 Hudson. Darrol was good with a wrench and had cool older brothers with cool older cars. I was…well, I really liked cars. When we went on to attend Stadium High School we all became members of the Steeds Car Club, a group likeminded teenage car nuts. By then we all owned cars, but go-karts were still very desirable and a bit exotic.

The first noticeable thing about the spring evening's event was the noise. Sandy's go-kart did not have a muffler and it was very loud. Releasing the exhaust explosions in the large concrete bowl resulted in the noise being extremely intensified. It sounded fantastic. We were sure that the neighborhood's residents were likely phoning the police and that soon we would be visited by the local authorities. Strangely we didn't care and luckily it didn't happen.

Next to the bowl was a tennis court that we used as our pit stop. The system was simple; we each slowly sipped our beers and waited our turn to blast around the dirt track at breathtaking speeds reaching nearly two digits. The track surrounded the football field so a couple of laps felt like a short but gratifying race. Then it was back to the "pits" to switch drivers and resume sipping on the slowly warming beer.

Yes, we were trespassing, drinking beer and disturbing the neighborhood's peace. We were also creating a cherished teenage memory while doing no real harm. The evening passed, the beer was gone and it was time to return the go-kart to Sandy's garage.

At the end of our senior year I signed my beer bowl buddies' yearbooks in a significant way: The yearbook contained a photo of the Stadium Bowl and on it I drew a little beer bottle with my name next to it.

My Other Mother

Mothers are held in high esteem, so much so that they have a day dedicated to them. On Mother's Day moms are wined and dined, given flowers and taken to the closest floral display or concert in the park. Dads have a day too, but it usually consists of being left alone in the garage for the day, then having the family around at dinner as he has second or third helpings of meatloaf without being scolded. Dads are fine with that, but moms are usually more celebrated and honored on their special day.

Phyllis & Rex Lambert (Mom & Dad) in 1956

As children most of us seem to have a preference for seeking comfort from our mothers over our fathers. This is very likely due to the life sustaining nourishment provided by our mothers from the moment one of dad's best performing sperm wigglers finds a good parking place in mom's egg shaped parking lot. We all know what happens for the next nine months (give-or-take a week or two), and then the new kid-on-the-block arrives tired, frightened, uncomfortable and, most likely, in need of a snack. The best place anyone can find themselves, under these circumstances, is in very close proximity to good ol' mommy.

Many reliable reports indicate that when we are finishing the last page of our life's book we often call out for our mothers. Yes, these ladies are indeed pretty special.

My mother had a style of parenting that frequently left me confused about what was going on between her ears, but I never questioned her love for me. She did her best and for that I am appreciative.

There was also a stepmother in my life, but I never lived with her. We had little contact and that was fine with both of us. There was not a problem between us, it was just understood that she was not taking on the role of being my mother. Jean signed on as my dad's new wife and, as far as I could observe, she did a great job of keeping him happy. Kudos to you Jean!

When Mother's Day rolls around each year, most people celebrate the woman who brought them into the world. As for me, I appreciate what my mother did for me, and I never questioned her love, but my appreciation goes beyond her. I have a number of "mothers" to celebrate. Let me name a few of them:

My best friend Bob's mom Margaret was always smiling and welcoming when I walked through her front door. Dale's mother Dorothy was very sarcastic and a bit intimidating, but, like her son, she was funny and kept me laughing with her smartass remarks. Duane's mom Mary always seemed happy when any of his friends arrived and she rarely failed to follow her greeting with the comment, "You boys want some toast?" The question was always asked with an uplifting lilt at the end of the question, almost sounding like she was singing rather than talking.

There were several other mothers that ranged from ghosts passing through a friend's house, barely noticed, to moms so beautiful that they looked as if they had just stepped out of a movie screen. My buddies and I didn't always stop by Patti's house just to visit Patti.

Of all the mothers in my young life, however, there was one who was very special: Ken's mother. But first I have to tell you about Ken and the rest of the family.

Ken Scott's 1965 graduation photo

Ken Scott and I became friends early in our sophomore year of high school. He was a friendly guy who possessed a sense of humor that appealed to every immature bone in my body. We both played trumpet in one of the school's bands, we both had an academic style that guaranteed we wouldn't be honored guests at any awards presentations, and we both sought out opportunities to have as much fun as any situation we were in would allow. He was a great guy and very popular with our classmates.

The friendship with Ken included many things. Together, with Ken on the guitar, we did a mean Everly Brothers vocal style rendition of the Kinks' song, "A Well Respected Man." Together we attended a few parties that, out of respect for his offspring and siblings, will not be detailed in this essay. The highest compliment that I can pay another male, as simple as this sounds, is, *He's really a good guy.* That was Ken.

Kayleen, one of Ken's three sisters, started high school when he and I began our junior year. She was a year younger and, like Ken, Kayleen was delightful to be around. She and I shared a table in Mr. Westlin's art class and in a short time we went from holding paint brushes in class to holding hands in the halls. Kayleen, unlike me, excelled at everything. She was very active academically and socially in school, and many of our teachers and classmates were confused as to why she decided that I was to be the recipient of her attention. It was a mystery to me too.

Lance and Kayleen attending a Stadium High School dance

Hanging out with Ken and Kayleen put me in touch with the rest of the Scott family. There were two additional siblings and a mom and dad. Younger sister Kathryn and older sister Karen were as much fun as the other "Ks" under the Scott's roof. Howard, sire of the Scott fold, was a harmonica playing trickster who had an infectious smile and a talent for teasing. Ruane was one of God's best examples of a perfect mother.

After a while, Kayleen and I parted as "steadies" but remained good friends. She was my first love and to this day she still owns a small piece of my heart.

The good news is that I continued to be a welcome guest at the Scott residence after our break-up. The great

news is that Ruane, mother of the Scott kids, and I seemed to grow closer than ever. I'm not alone in having this feeling. Ruane was *that mom*, the one who makes everyone feel that he or she is the most important person in the world when in her presence.

Ruane & Howard Scott

On many occasions she provided a few words of wisdom and support that got me through minor, and sometimes more difficult times, like my high school graduation.

Graduating from high school was one of my early successes in life. For me academics had been difficult and every summer I was provided the opportunity to retake a class that I'd failed to pass during the school year.

Walking across the stage and receiving my diploma during the graduation ceremony made me feel like I'd been rescued from a ship that was on the verge of sinking. At the close of the ceremony I sought out some recognition from my family members, but they had decided to leave the event early. There I stood, alone amongst hundreds of classmates that were being hugged by parents and siblings. I scanned the area looking for my family, not knowing that they had already gone home. It was one of the saddest and loneliest moments of my life.

A short distance away stood Ken, surrounded by his parents and sisters, each taking their turn to give him a congratulatory hug. It was then that Ruane saw me through the crowd, standing alone. She stepped away from her family and walked up to me. Her comments were brief but full of love, and were followed by a long hug. I no longer felt alone.

The years after high school were filled with the typical highs and lows of a young man maturing, but for the most part they were enjoyable. There were dozens of times during that period when I wanted to see Howard and Ruane, to seek out their wisdom and advice, or to just enjoy the comfort of being with them. A phone call always resulted in an invitation to stop by for a visit.

My most cherished memory of Ruane is of a simple day spent with her. I went to her home and she invited me to stay for the rest of the day. It was going to be just the two of us and I felt so honored that she was giving me so much of her time. We talked, had a meal together and then climbed into my 1957 Buick for a casual cruise in the old and elegant car. We enjoyed the passing scenery, took care of a few errands for her and then did something that seemed so "Ruane" to me.

"What music are the kids listening to now?" she asked.

At that time Carol King's *Tapestry* album was a huge hit, so that is what we went to the record store for her to purchase. We returned to her home, put the record on the turntable and quietly listened to both sides.

That day was one of the best days of my life.

Ruane passed away several years ago. Unfortunately I

was not able to be with her near the end. A week or two after her passing I had a vivid dream. Unlike most dreams that are odd and for the most part unrealistic, this dream was simple and seemed like it was actually happening in reality. I was standing in an area void of details when Ruane quietly appeared. No words were spoken between us. She walked up to me, looked into my eyes and smiled, then gave me a tight hug that lasted for a long time. I like to think that it really was her and that she came to say goodbye.

Tragedy on Tanglewood

As I begin writing this story my 70th birthday is a few weeks away, and I find myself reflecting on some of the successes and failures in my life. At the top of the failure list is something that happened to me on the warm night of June 11, 1965. It is without question the most embarrassing experience thus far in my life.

My graduation from Stadium High School was held at the University of Puget Sound Field House. Several hundred students and I marched up the aisles and onto the stage to be handed our diplomas and sent off into our futures. For some of us our immediate future was the "Senior Class Party" that was being held that evening after the graduation ceremony was completed.

STADIUM HIGH SCHOOL

Graduation Exercises

Friday, June 11, 1965

University of Puget Sound Field House
8:00 p.m.

N⁰ 1665   Admission - 50c

The party was sponsored by the school's administration and would be held on Tanglewood Island, a small piece of land in Puget Sound where a resort was located. This facility included a ballroom where the participating students were to spend all night dancing and, under strict supervision, partying. Absolutely no alcoholic beverages were allowed, and we were not to leave the building or the landscaped areas around the building.

I had no intention of attending this party because the $15 charge was well beyond my budget, and besides, a few of my best friends were driving to the ocean after graduation with the intent of partying without any supervision. That plan had sounded fine to me until a friend offered to pay my way to the senior class party. I was surprised by the offer, but, considering the person extending the invitation, I accepted. Bobbiejean Purgatorio was a good friend, one of the prettiest girls at school and one of the funniest people that I'd ever met. I accepted her generous offer knowing that her sense of humor would guarantee a great experience.

Bobbiejean getting ready for the graduation ceremony

My three years at Stadium High School included a limited amount of musical endeavors. I played trumpet in the school band for two years and also played the tenor saxophone briefly with a few classmates who had pooled their talents and were attempting to be a rock & roll band called the Castlemen. I had also rehearsed a few times with friend Vernon Clark's band, the Soul Set. With that group I was doing my best to learn how to become a lead vocalist. They were kind enough to let me sit in with them, but they didn't ask me to become a member of the band. Remember this paragraph because it contains some vital facts that contributed to my almost needing therapy after the senior class party.

The graduation ceremony portion of the evening had come to an end. We had marched across the stage, received our "sheep skins" and then mingled with family and friends for congratulatory hugs and handshakes. Some of the fresh graduates left for home, some headed for various parties, and the majority prepared to leave for the all-night party on Tanglewood Island.

We were loaded into waiting buses, driven several miles to a waterfront dock and lined up to board a surplus World War II amphibious landing craft. It was one of the big flat-bottomed boxes with wheels seen approaching the beaches of Normandy in wartime footage. Referred to as a "Duck" by soldiers, this watercraft waiting to transport us across the short distance was sparse on luxury but spacious on capacity. I don't recall how many of us fit in it, or how many loads of us were taken from shore to shore, but I do recall there being a lot of teenagers spending the night at the resort.

We were dropped off about 10:00 p.m. and were to be picked back up at 7:00 a.m. the following morning. At the resort we were provided a large ballroom, an area for snacks, and a few bathrooms. There was a band playing much of the night and the newly graduated students were expected to dance and party well into the wee hours and, if necessary, find a spot on a bench or the floor to sleep until it was time to return home in the morning. There were chaperones everywhere, and no one was allowed to leave the immediate area. The grounds around the building were patrolled by parents and teachers who took their guard duty very seriously. The event seemed a bit like spending the night at Alcatraz.

Bobbiejean and I were hanging out together and doing our share of dancing to the music provided by the entertainment, the Washington Combo. Late into the night the band took a break and someone called out, "Let the Castlemen play! Let them use your instruments!" The combo members were receptive to the request with the exception of the saxophone player. Understandably, he declined my request to use his saxophone, likely because he didn't want my slobber all over the saxophone's mouthpiece and reed. I

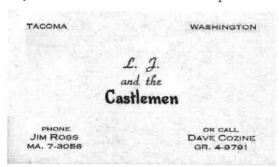

left the bandstand frustrated that my Castlemen classmates were going to get a few minutes of student stardom and I'd be left out. It was time to get creative!

Friend Vernon Clark, a member of the Soul Set band, was standing nearby on the dance floor. I seized the opportunity to solicit his help in getting me on stage with the Castlemen. I reminded him that I'd rehearsed with his band and that he, no doubt, thought I had a fine set of vocal chords. I put my arm around his shoulders and said, "Go up and tell the band that I've been singing with your group and that I'm really good!"

Vernon, either being a supportive friend or seeing the opportunity to witness my vocal Titanic hit an iceberg, did as I requested. My former band-mates called out, "Lance, come on up and sing with us."

This was it. I'd been singing along to records in my bedroom for a year or two and had practiced with the Soul Set twice. I was ready for my public debut. Yes, the crowd before me, many of whom I'd known since kindergarten, were about to witness the official beginning of my enormously successful career of emoting vocally into a microphone. I may have arrived with Bobbiejean, but it was likely that I'd be leaving with dozens of adoring young ladies who had swooned and nearly fainted when they heard the sound of velvety beauty that left my throat and filled the ballroom during my never-to-be-forgotten display of vocal perfection. Yes, this is what I was hoping for but, sadly, it did not turn out exactly as I had envisioned.

The crowd was excited to see their classmates on stage and anticipated some good rock & roll. A quick discussion among the Castlemen resulted in the choice of the song *Money* to be performed. It was a song I'd memorized and felt confident would be easy to belt out as well as any version heard on local jukeboxes. It all went well until I opened my mouth.

The band started off perfectly and the opening bars of the popular song began creating smiling faces and swaying bodies in the audience. The moment arrived for me to begin singing the first verse. I'd quote the lyrics here, but then I'd have to pay a royalty to the song's publisher. Let's just say that the lyrics refer to a preference for cash over things that are acquired at no cost. I missed my cue so the band played on until the appropriate moment to begin singing again arrived. Noise did begin coming out of my mouth but, unfortunately, it did not sound like the Castlemen and I were performing the same song. I was so badly off key that the band stared at me in amazement and stopped playing. The audience was also staring at me as if I'd just stabbed a cat in front of them. It became extremely quiet in that large room. I sheepishly asked the band to start again. This time around I was in the proper key and all was going well for about four seconds before the evening's second musical disaster happened. As I was "singing," it became obvious that I was still in a transitional period in my life in which my voice was changing from a boy's to a young man's. The sound emitting from my mouth suddenly cracked like a baseball bat hitting a bowling ball.

Up to this point the audience and band members had been tolerant and even hopeful that I'd regain control and provide them with a performance to tell their grandchildren about. Instead, I became the favorite comedy act of the night. It appeared that everyone in the room began laughing. Even the chaperones could not contain themselves. I stood there completely humiliated, and also aware that at the same moment my closest buddies were at the ocean drinking beer, laughing and standing around a blazing campfire while intentionally singing off-key.

Now what do I do? I mumbled something into the microphone about having too much to drink and did my best imitation of being drunk as I fake stumbled off the stage. It was about 2:00 a.m. at this point and I was not going to be able to face anyone for the rest of the night, or perhaps for the rest of my life. I continued stumbling out of the ballroom and out of the building. Bobbiejean, bless her big heart, followed me and assured me that it was not as bad as I thought. She meant well but she was a poor liar.

We made our way into the basement of the building and found a stack of small rowboats. Several were stacked up within each other like drinking glasses in a cabinet. We climbed into a boat at the top of a stack and hid from everyone until it was time to leave in the morning.

I avoided eye contract with everyone as we left the resort and made our way to the waiting landing craft. This extremely embarrassing experience was going to take some time to recover from, if ever.

There is almost a happy ending to this story. My friends knew how badly I felt and most of them had the decency to not bring up the senior party catastrophe again. Well, almost everyone. I have remained close friends with most of my classmates and still see many of them often. At a party many years ago classmate John Dammeier walked up to me as the song *Money* was being played. He looked at me and said, "Hey Lance, sing *Money*." Enough time had passed that I did not burst into tears and, instead, laughed along with him.

Did the memory of this musical disaster fade away? No, it did not. At our high school's 35th reunion several of my classmates walked up to me and in unison called out, "Lance, sing *Money* for us!" I was still embarrassed but I laughed. Another classmate, Mark Petersen, suggested, prior to our 40th class reunion, that I rehearse with his band. They were booked to perform at the reunion and he thought that a second attempt at singing *Money* in front of our classmates might repair the psychological damage that resulted from the first attempt. This seemed too much of a risk and I declined his offer.

Did I ever sing in public again? Yes, and I think I sounded pretty good, but I'd prefer if you do not ask the opinion of anyone who was in the audience.

About the Author

Lance Lambert lives in Seattle where he spends his time writing books, producing & hosting television and radio programs, participating in storytelling events, going to car shows and trying to be a good husband, father, grandfather and friend. So far most of the reviews have been favorable.

Also By
Lance Lambert

Fenders, Fins & Friends: Confessions of a Car Guy

"Read this and you will gain insight into a down-to-earth soul, with a big heart, and an entertaining way of seeing the world."

Theresa Poalucci, Publisher
Journal Newspapers

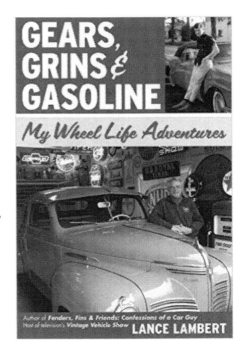

Gears, Grins & Gasoline: My Wheel Life Adventures

"Lance Lambert's second book is wonderful... a new look into the life of one of America's quintessential car guys... I found it engaging and it would not allow me to put it down... "

David Dickinson
Author & Historian
The Old Car Nut Book series

Made in the USA
San Bernardino, CA
04 August 2017